MANDALA
COLORING BOOK
LOVE AND HEART

THIS BOOK BELONGS TO

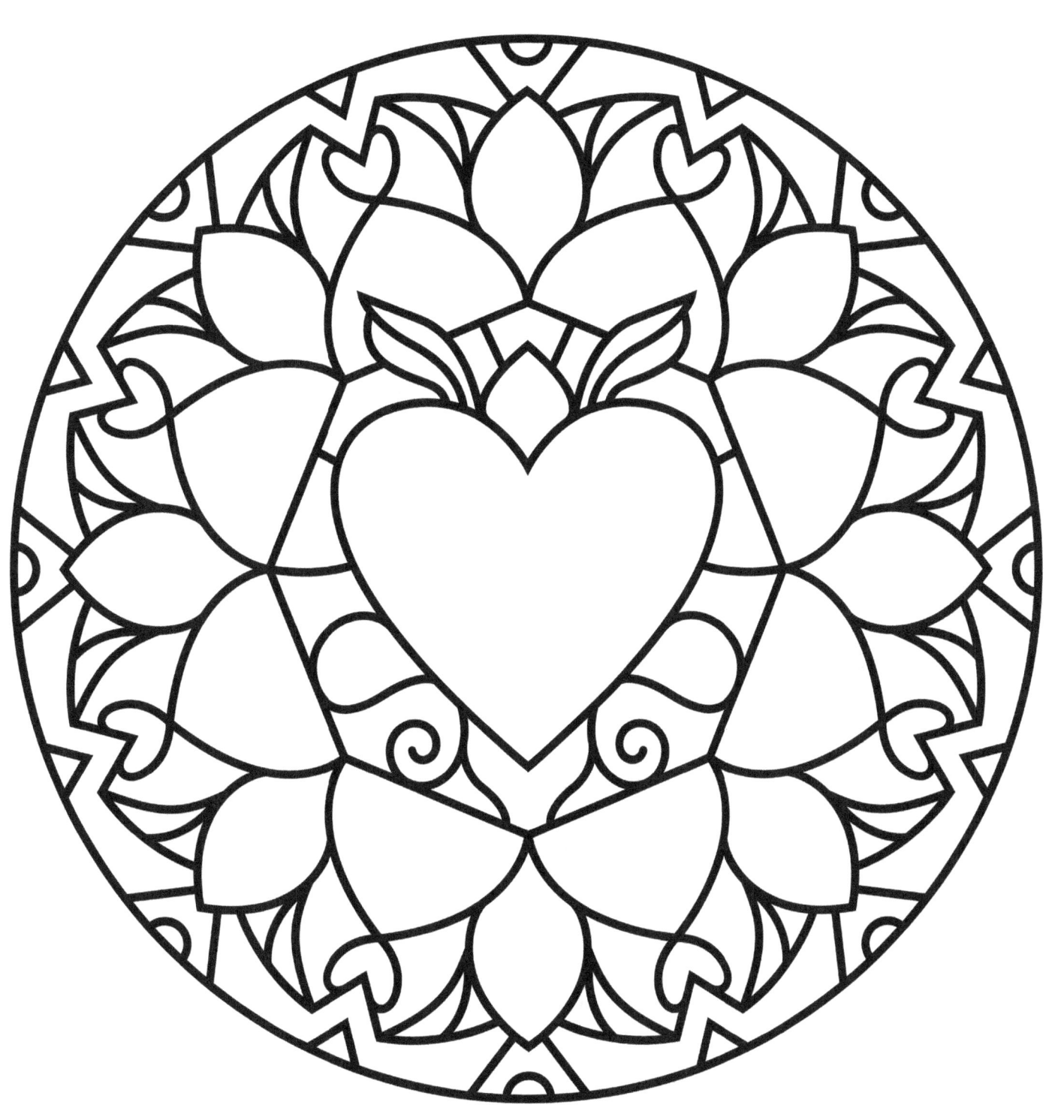

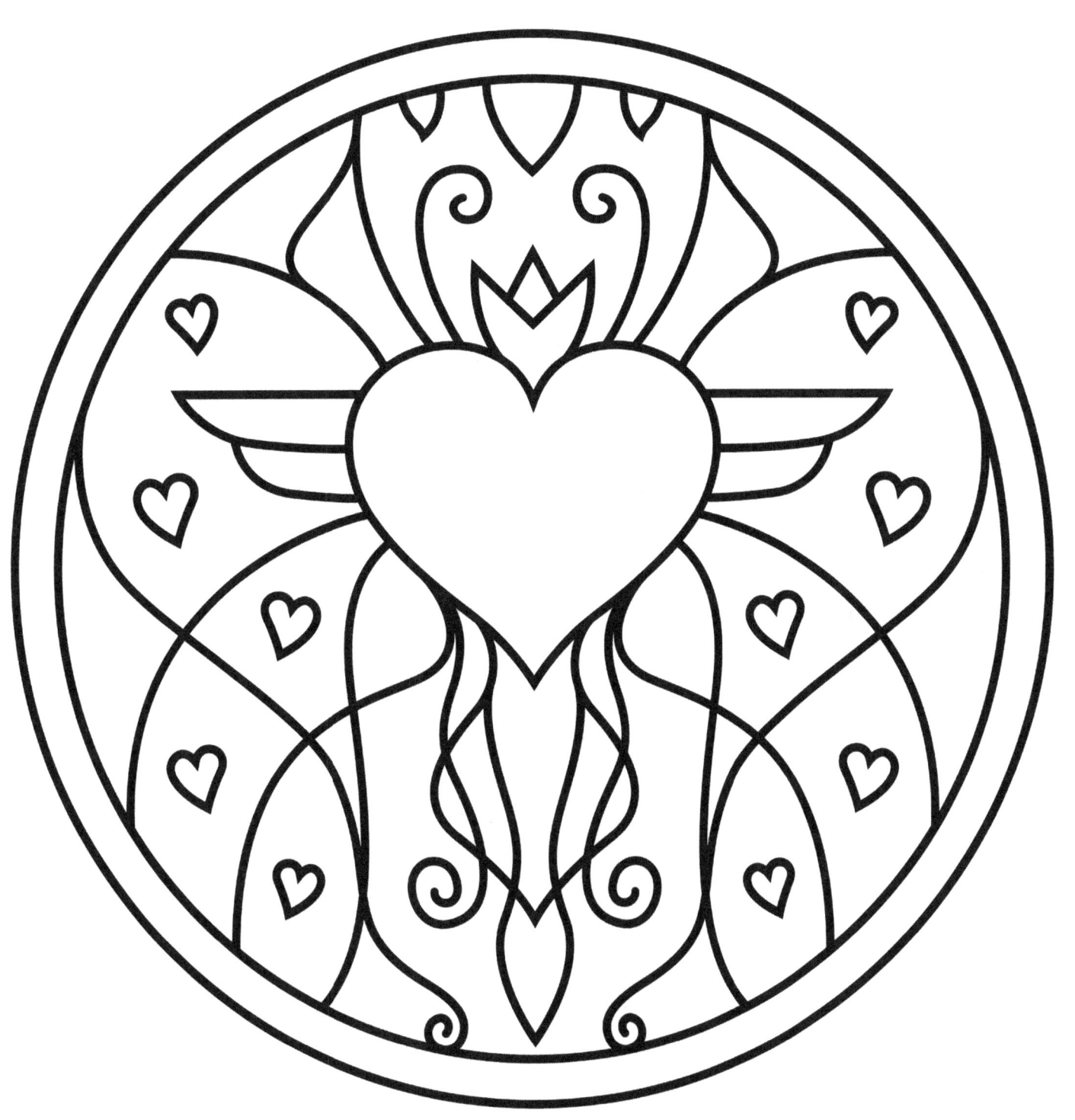

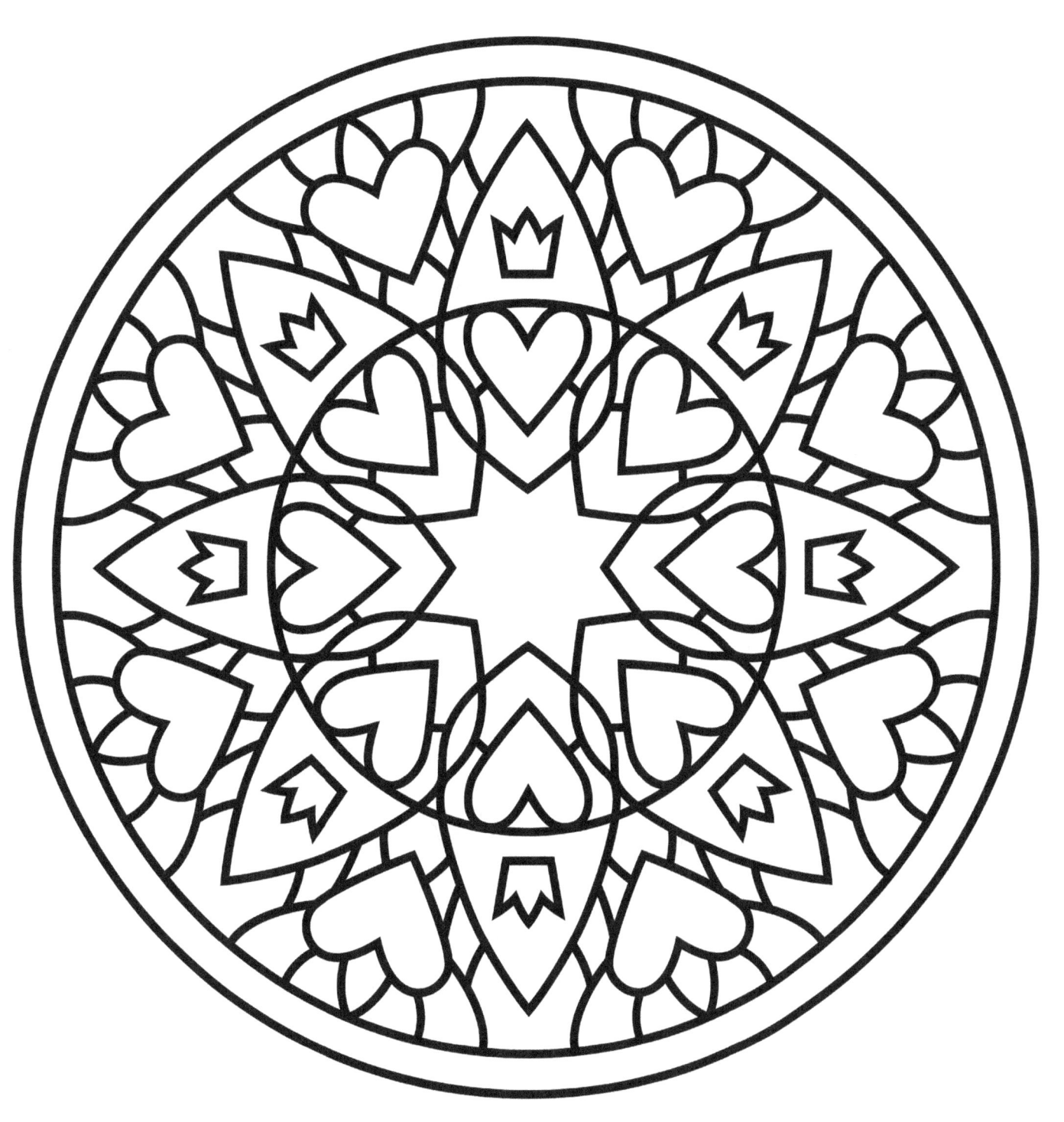

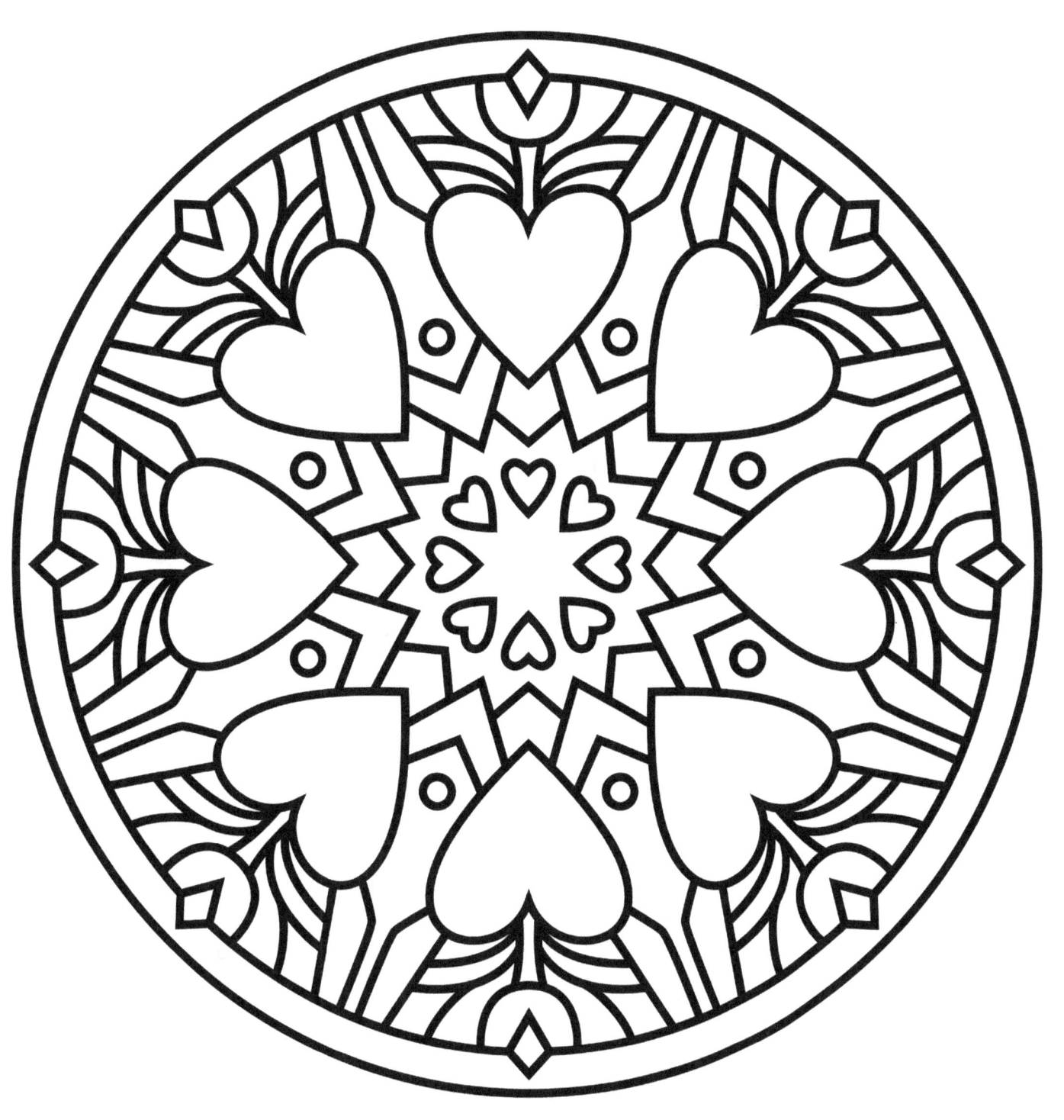

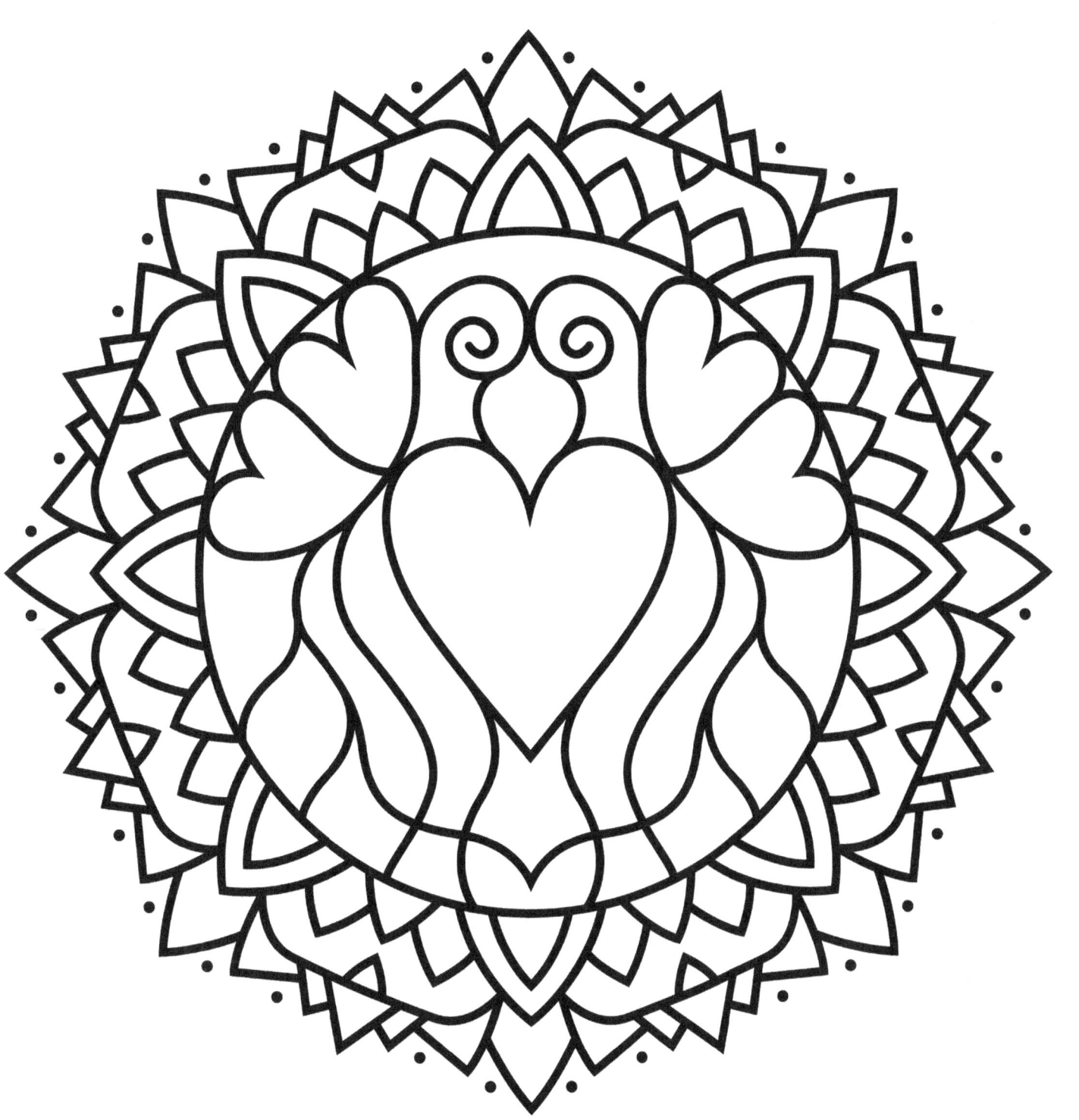

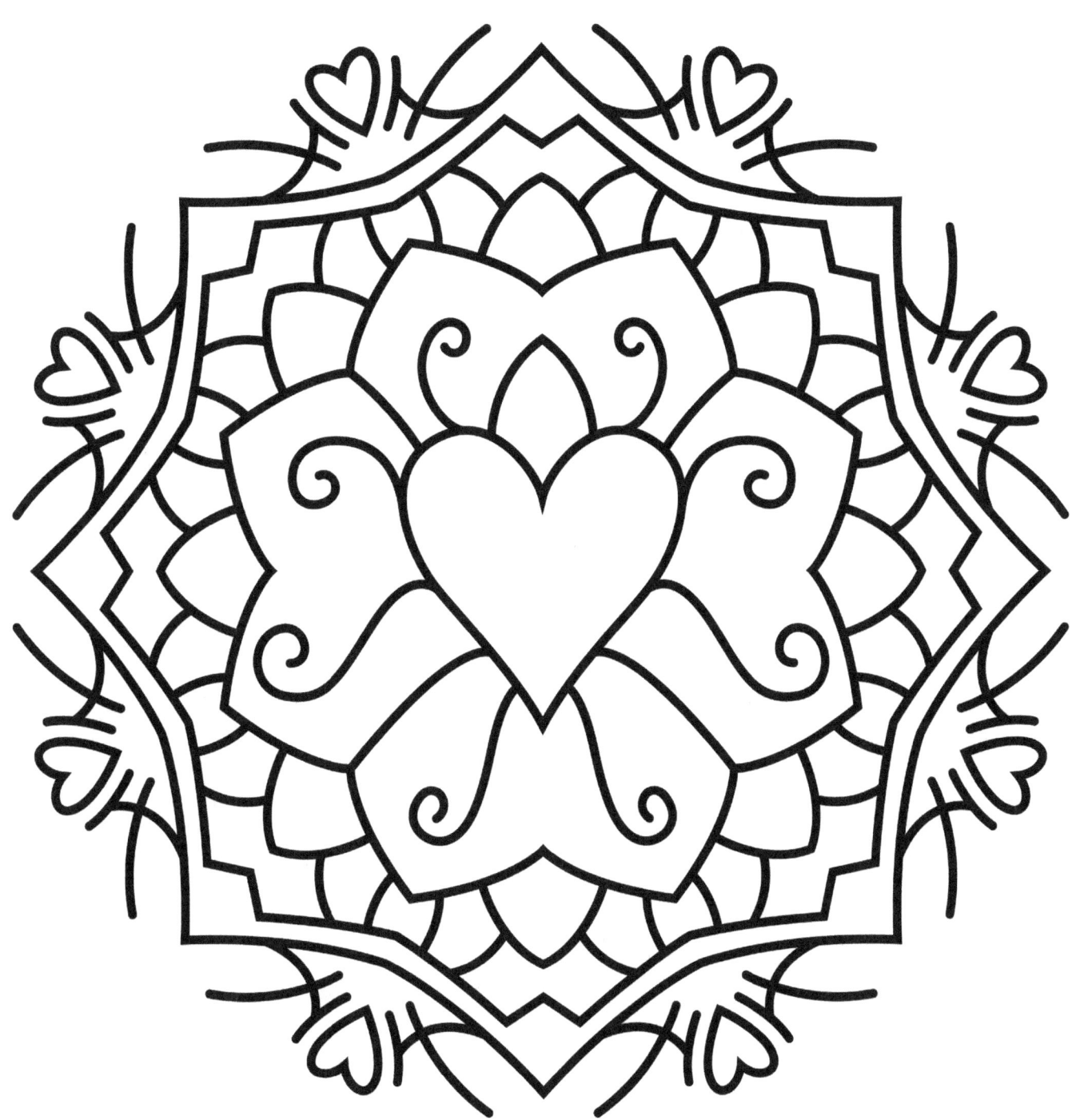

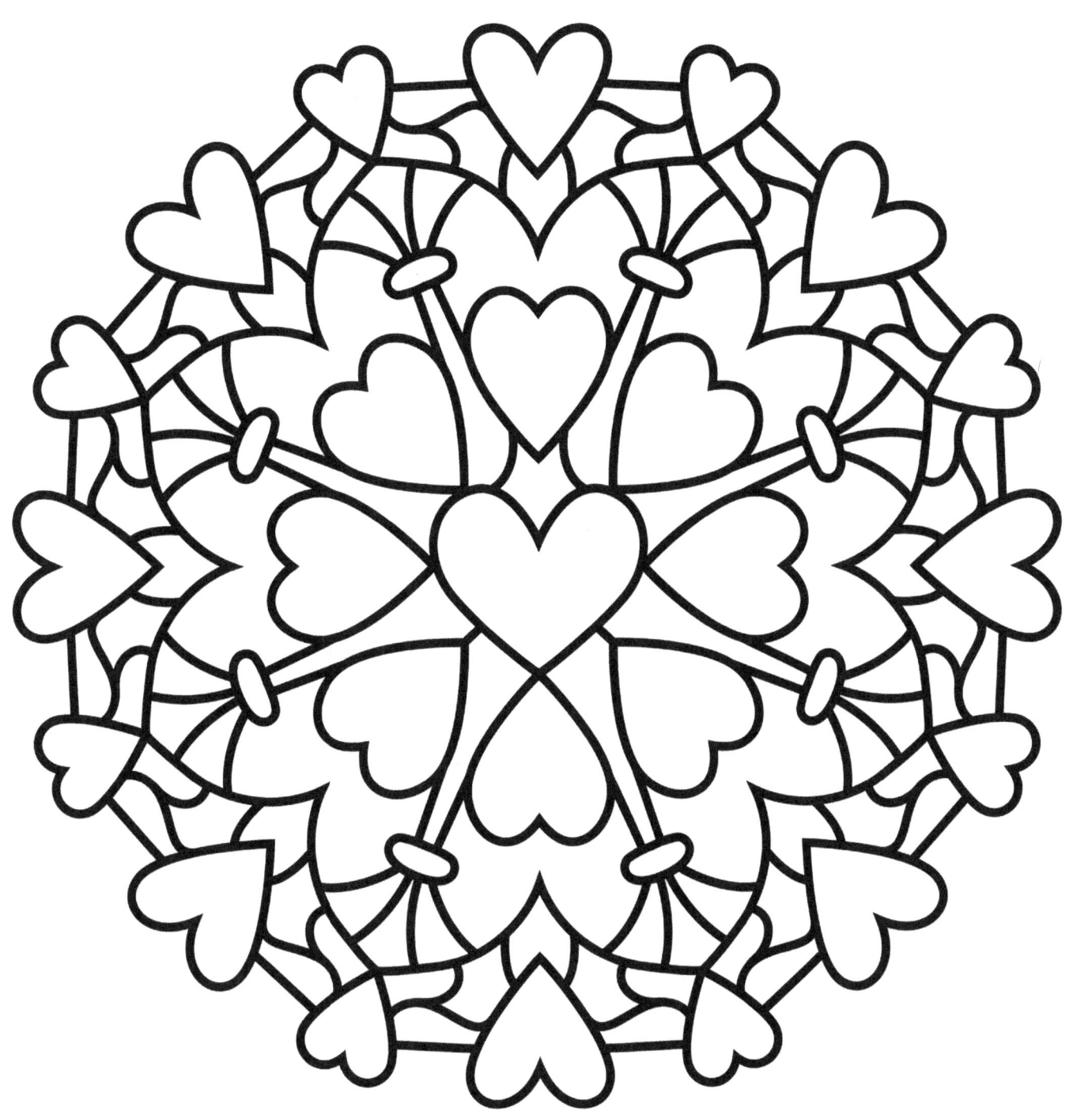

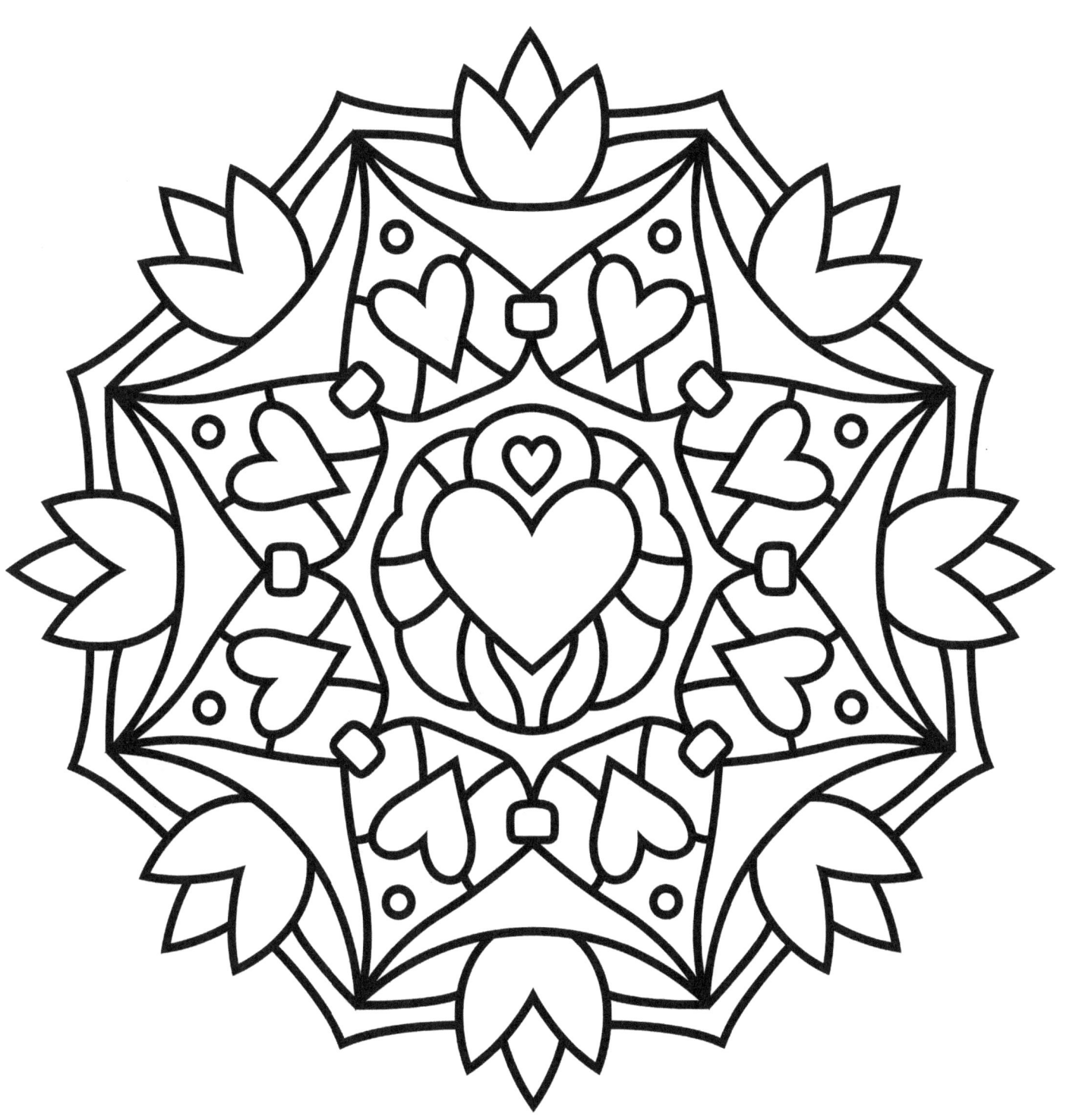

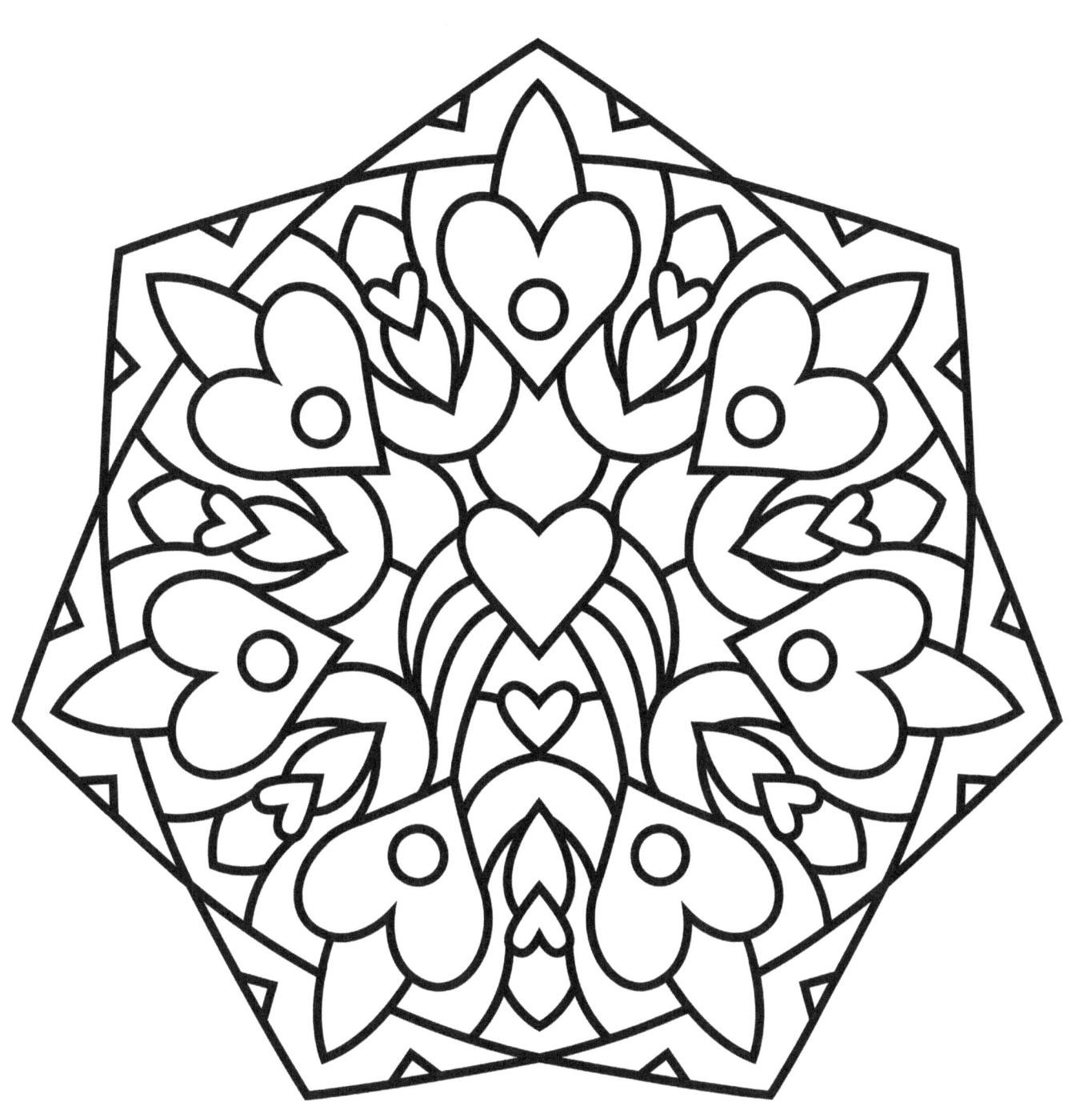

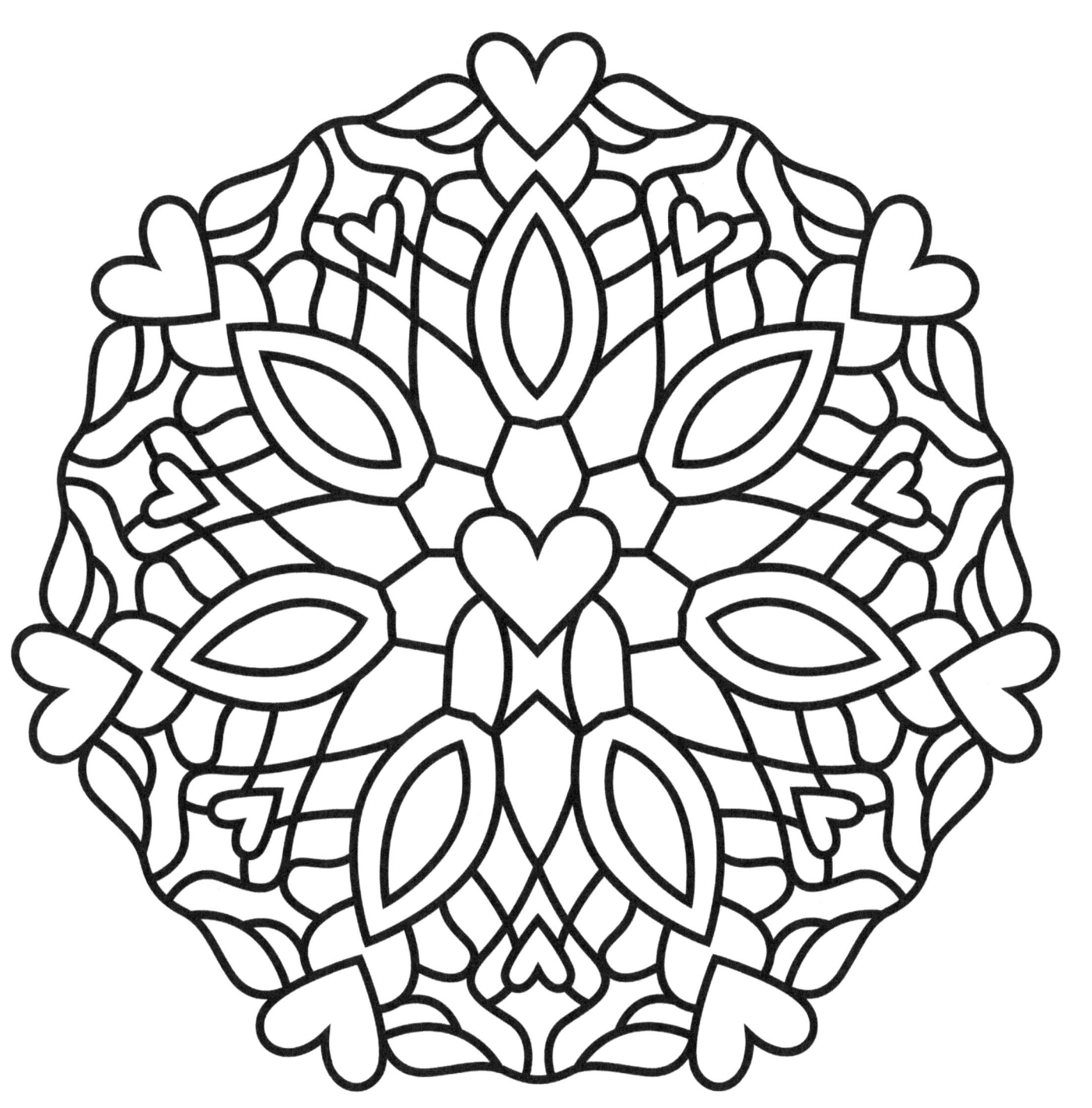

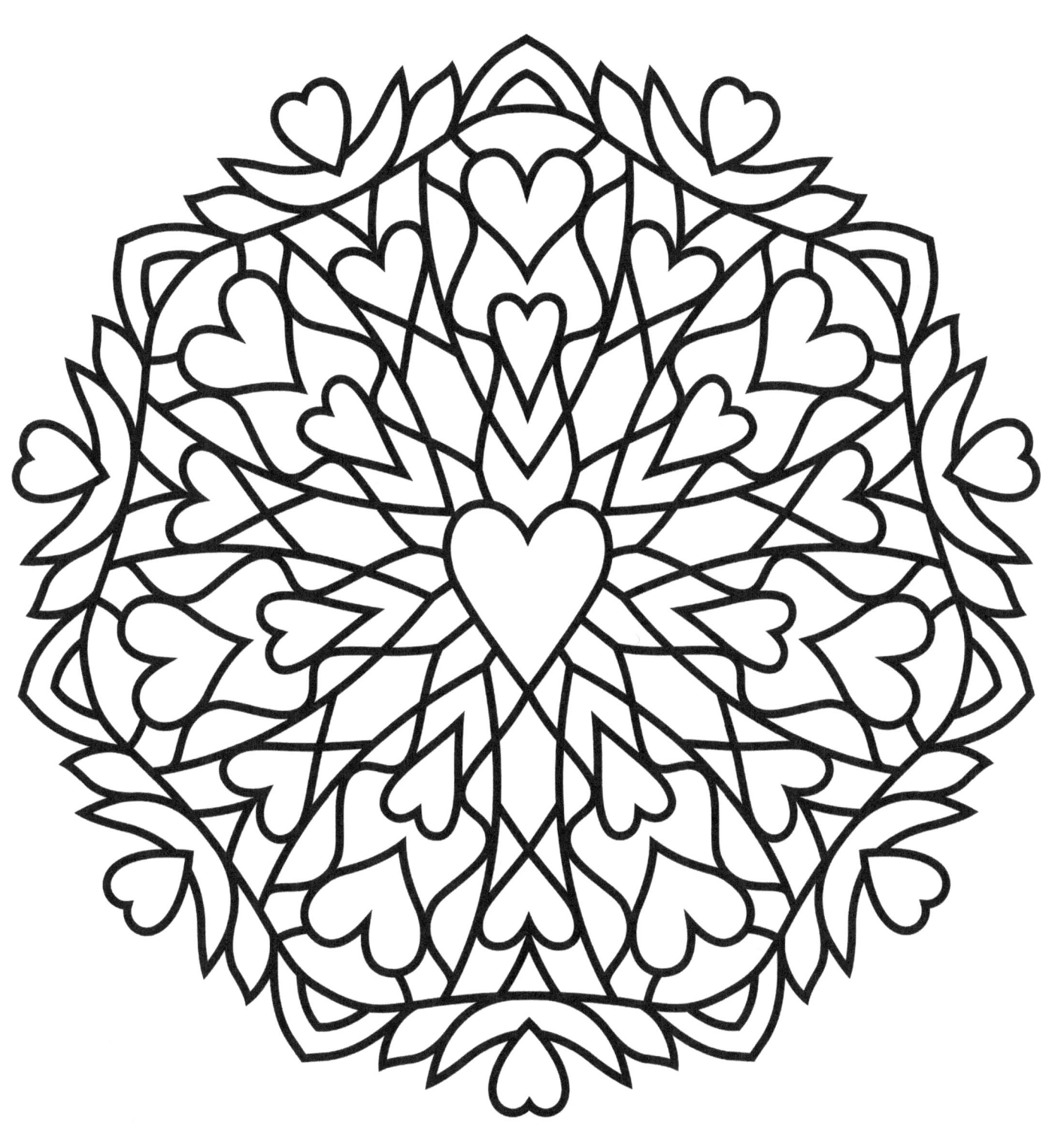

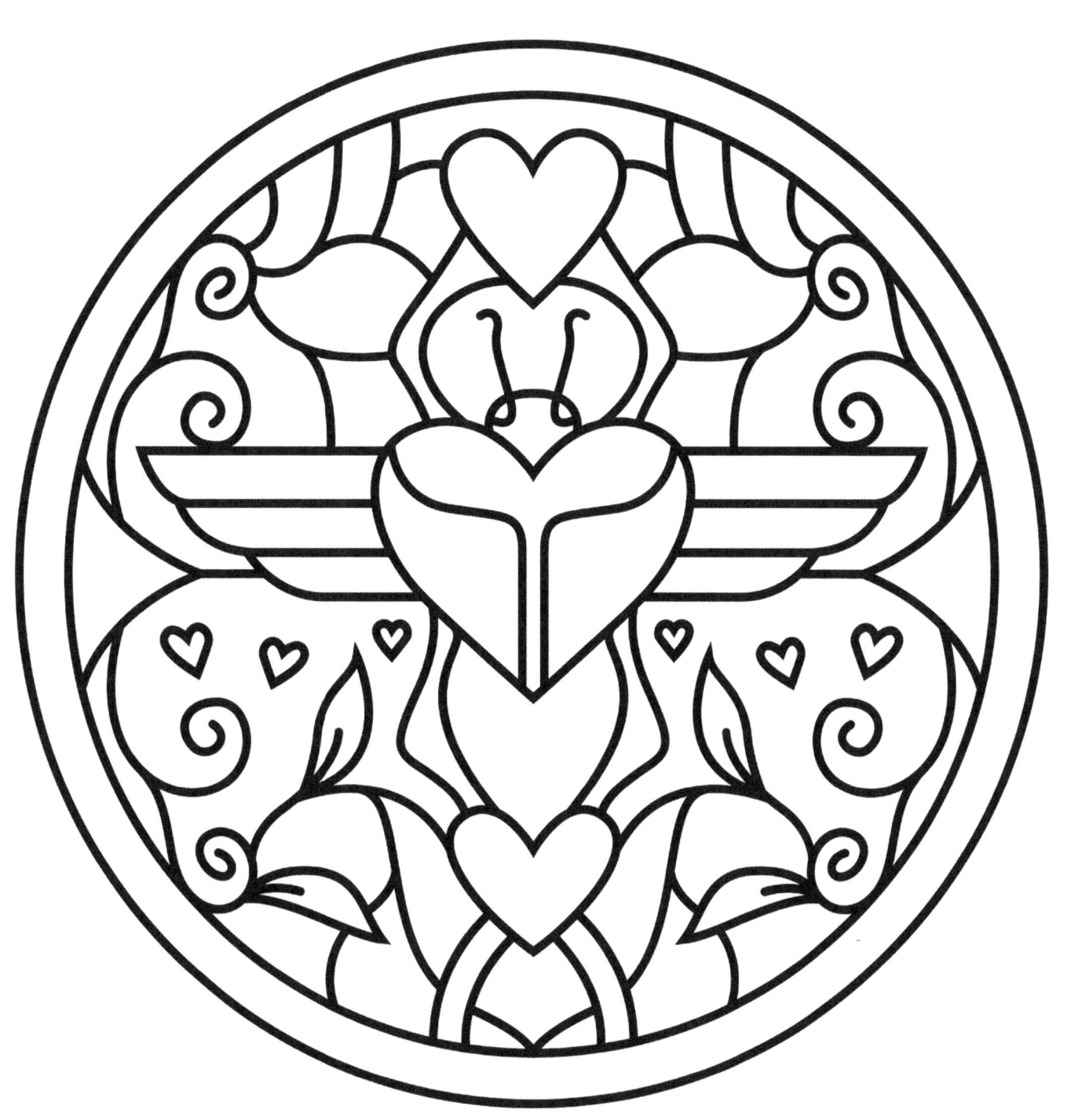

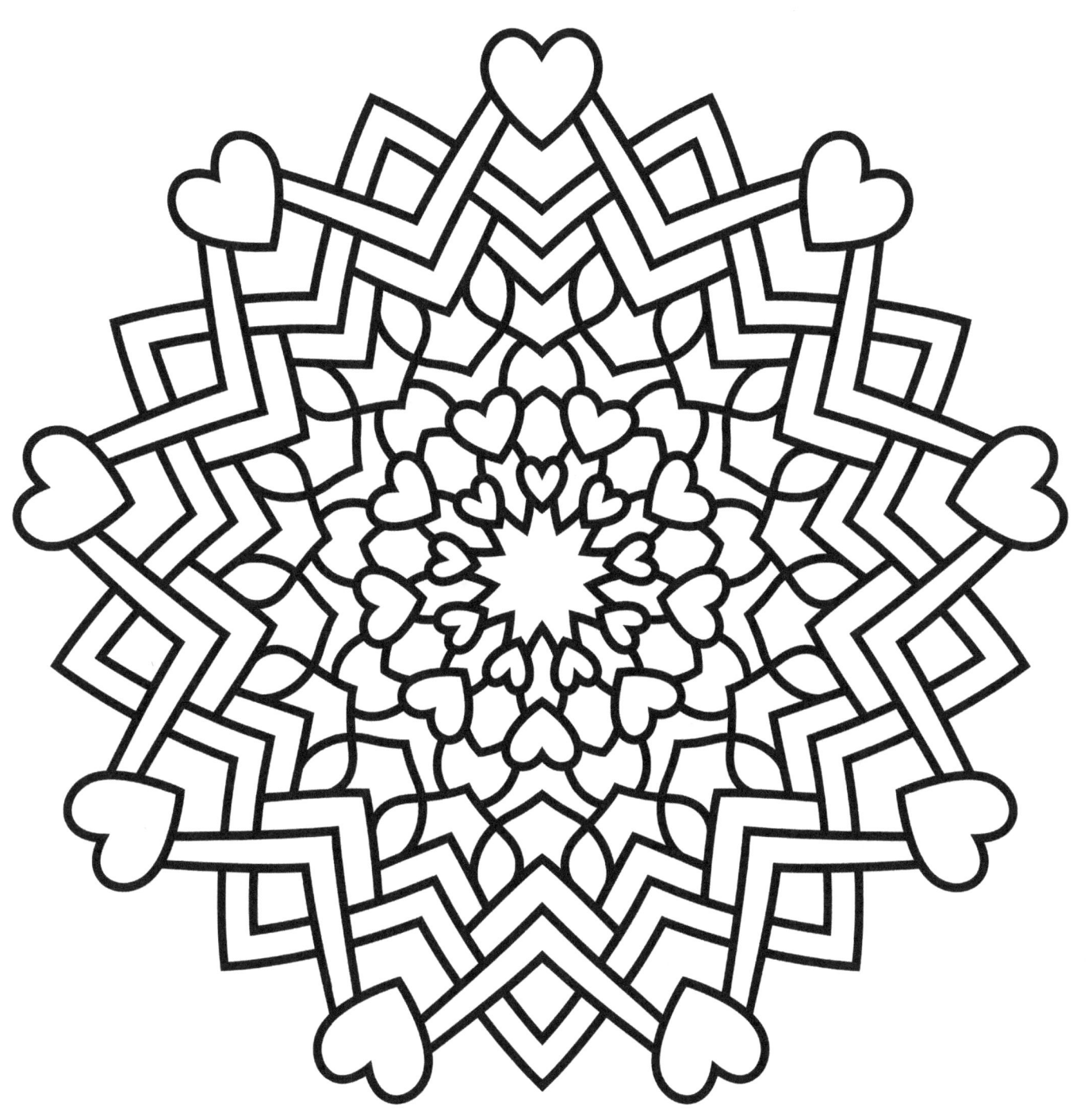

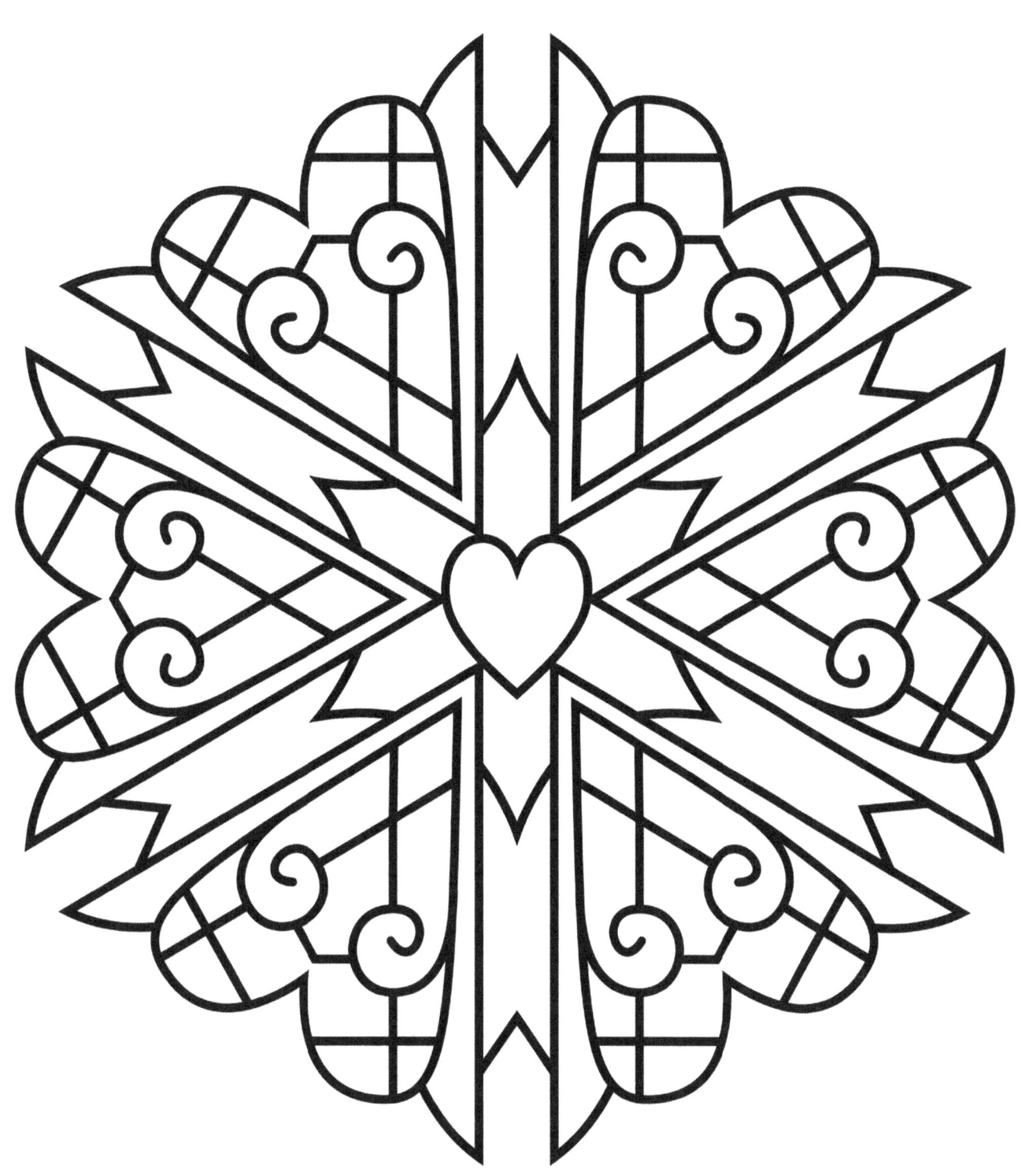

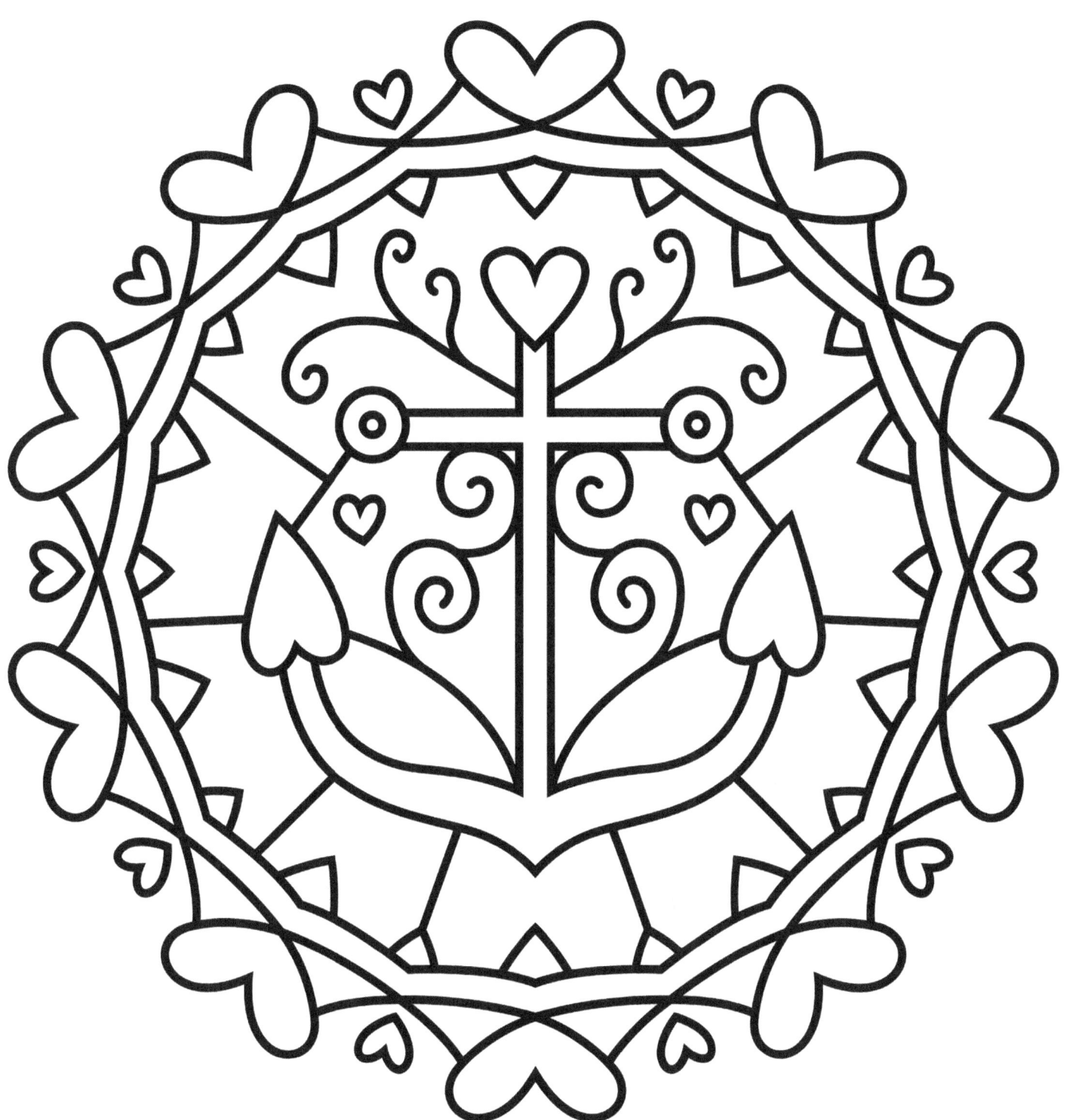

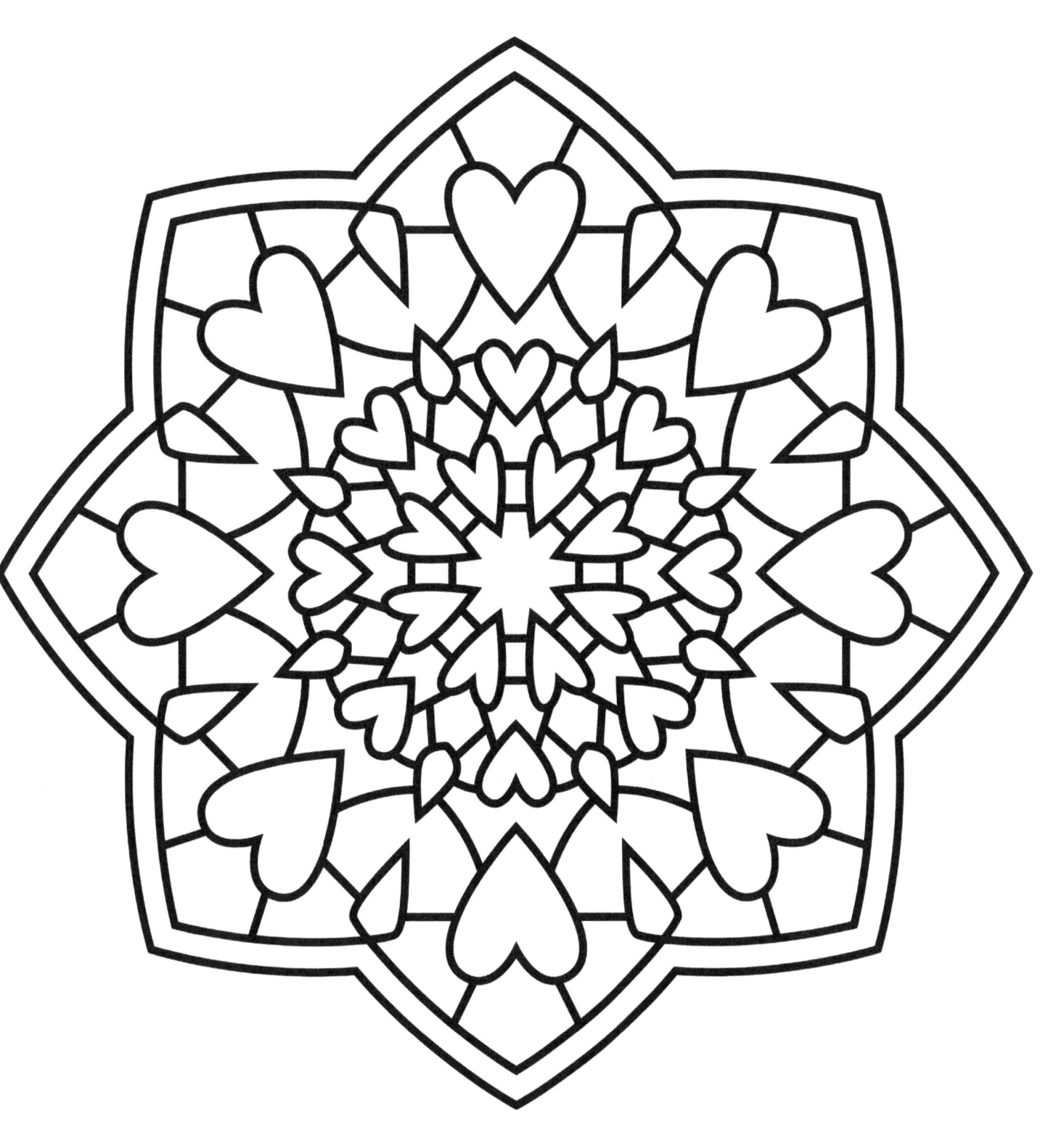

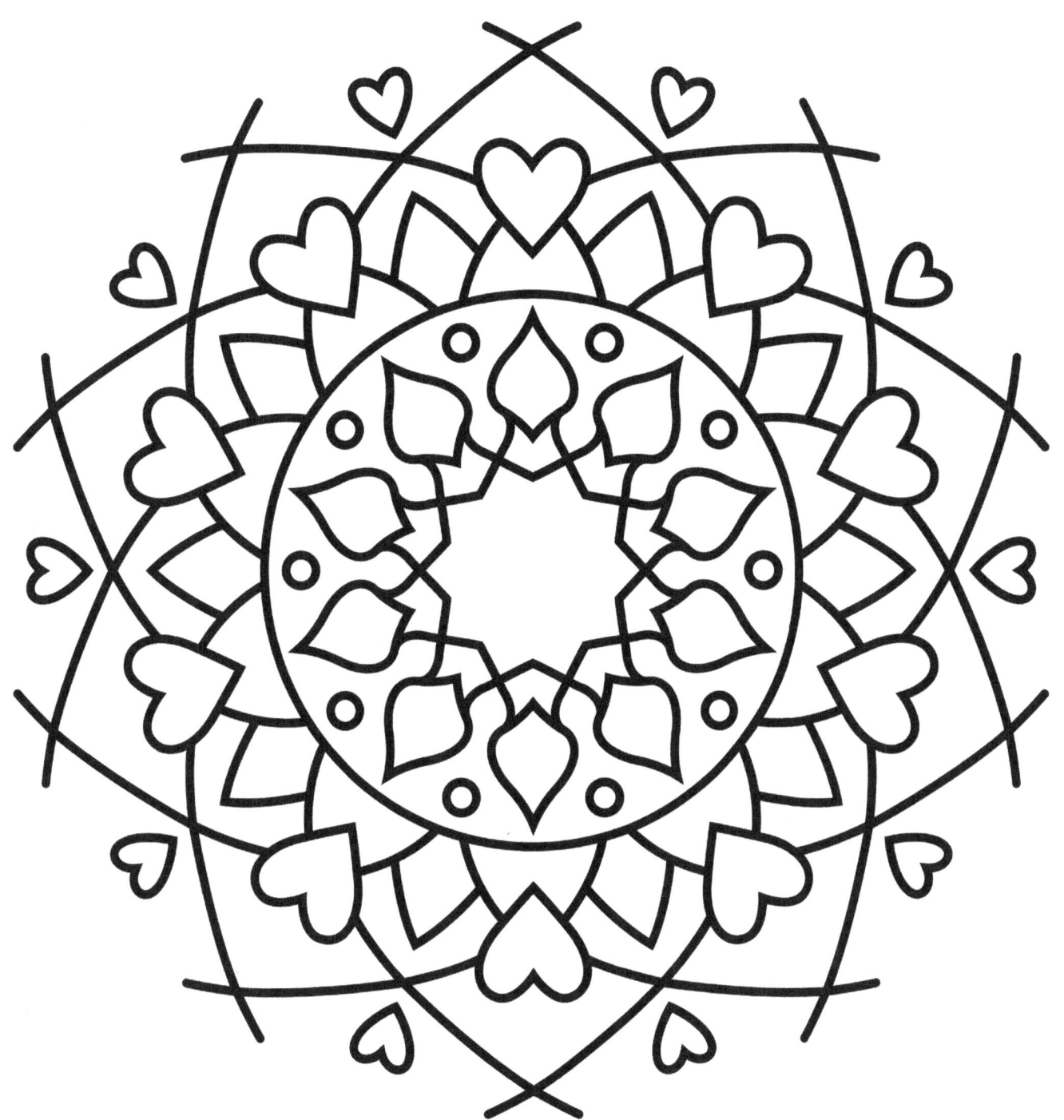

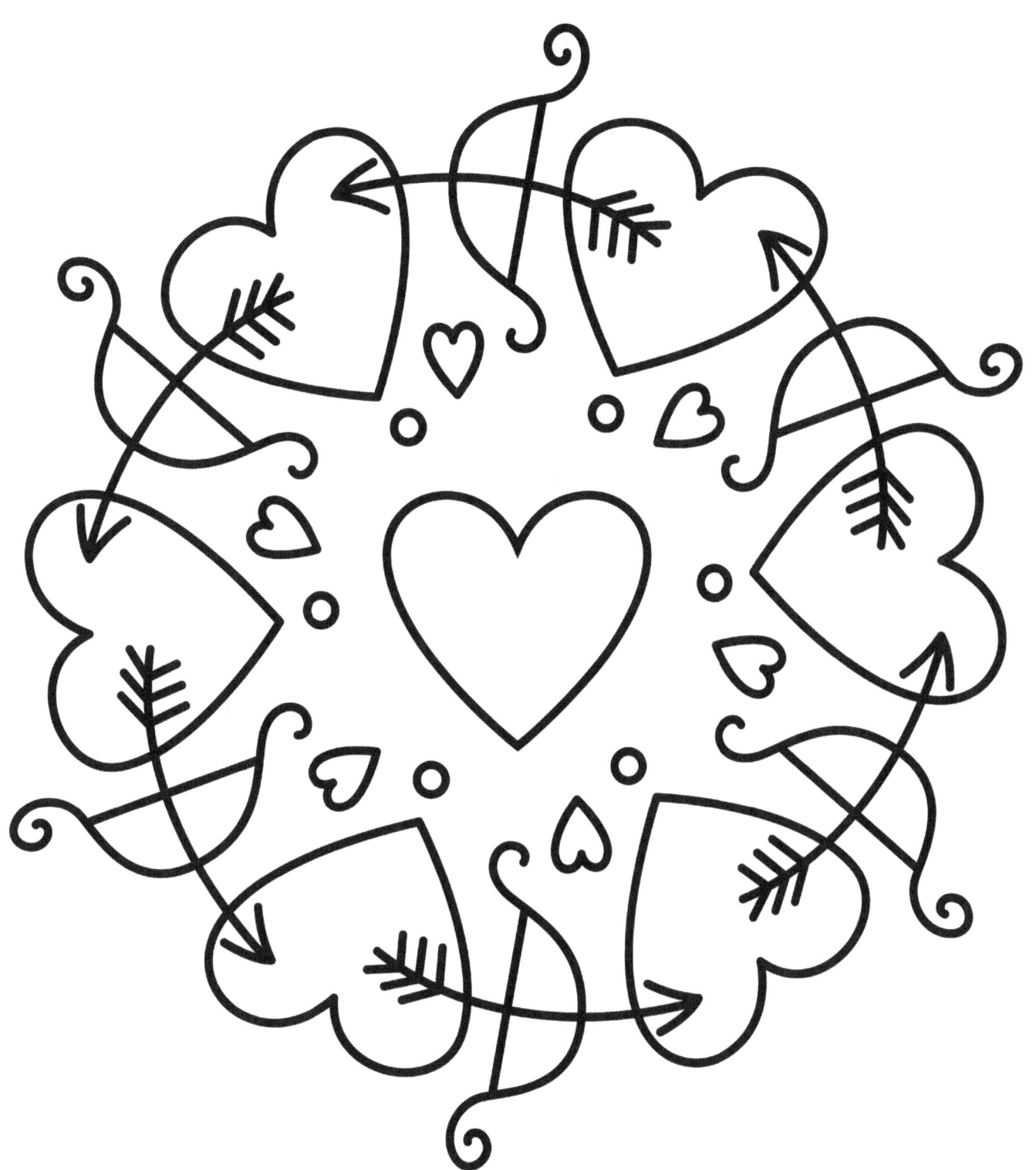

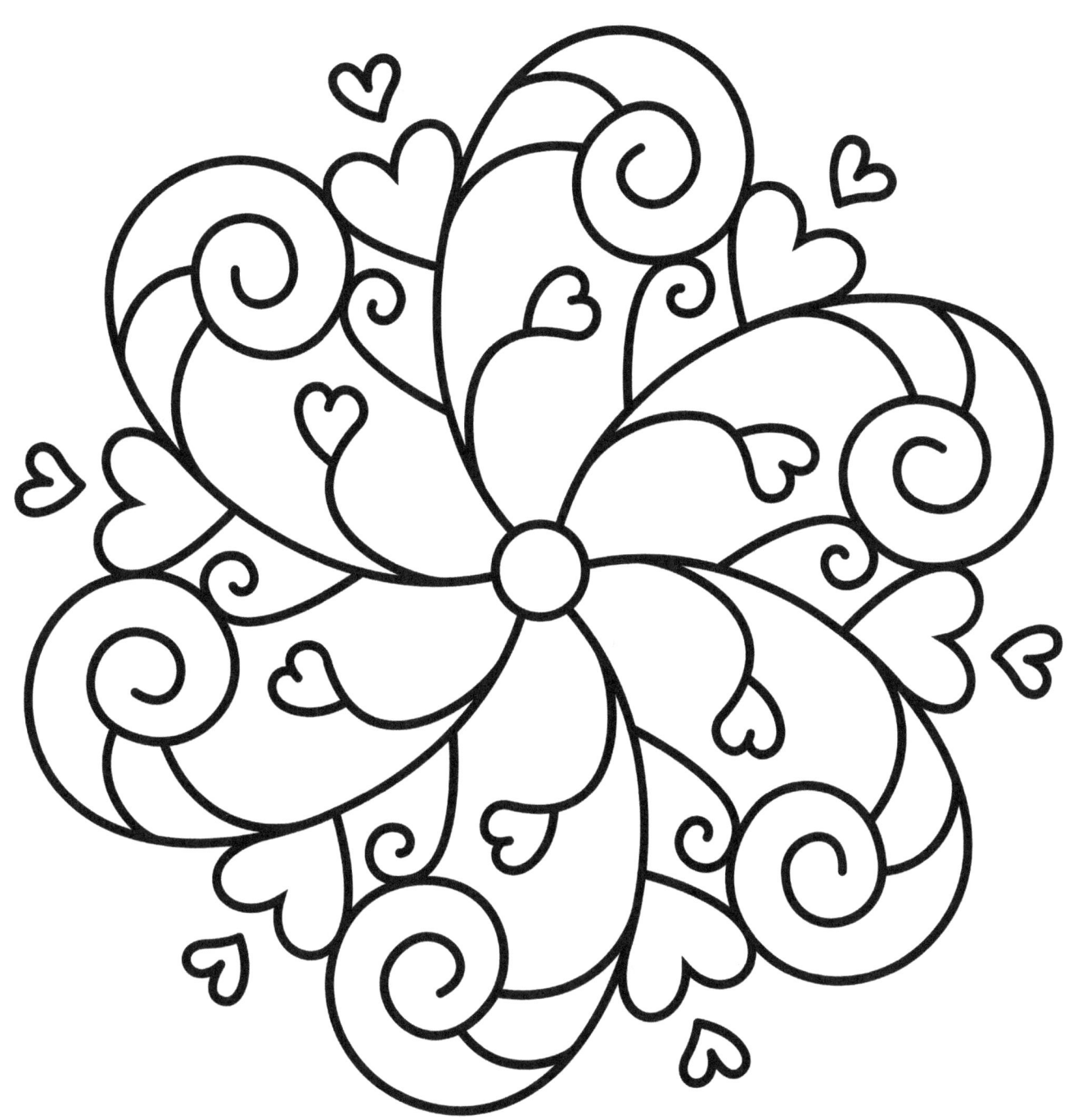

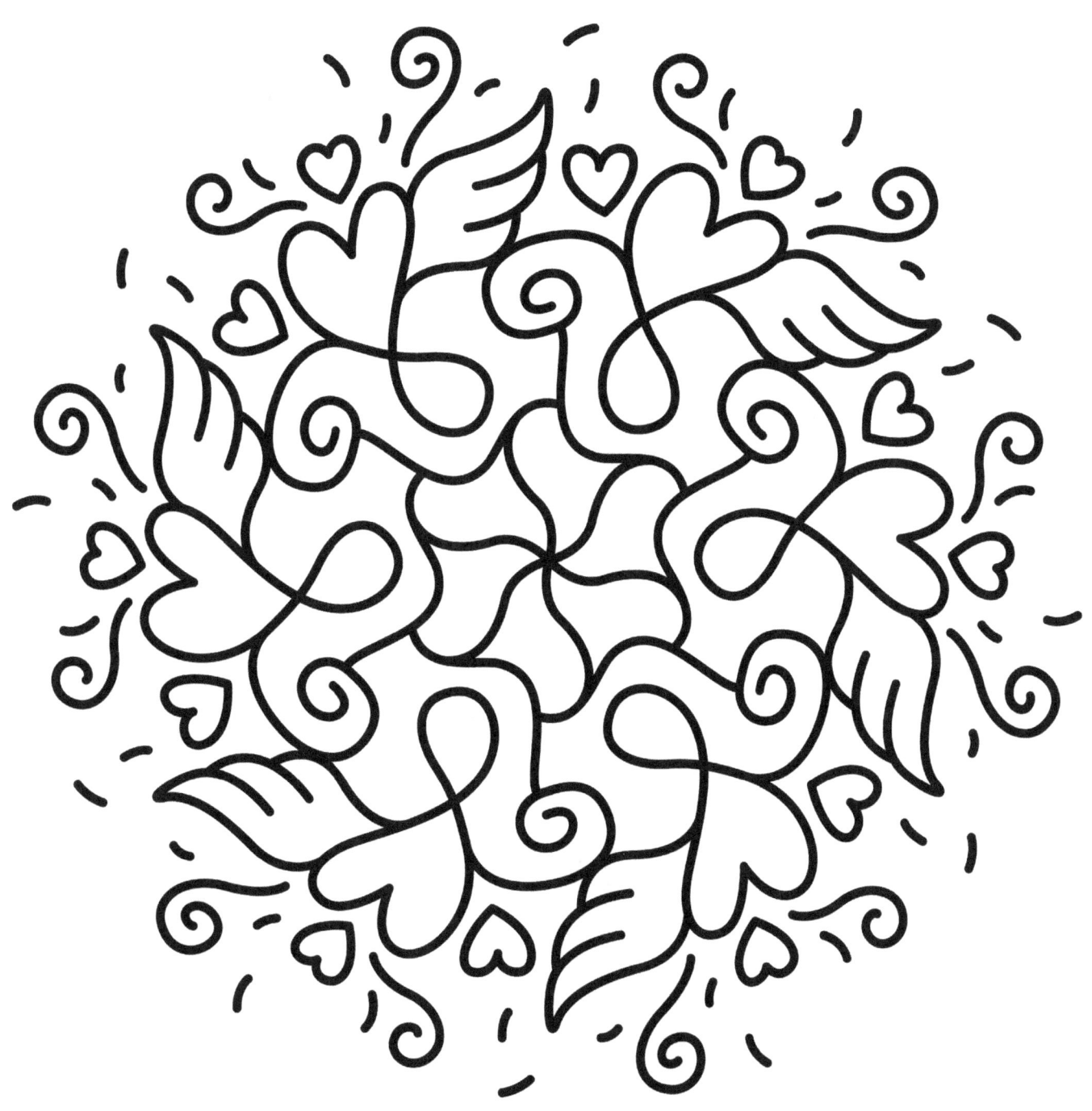

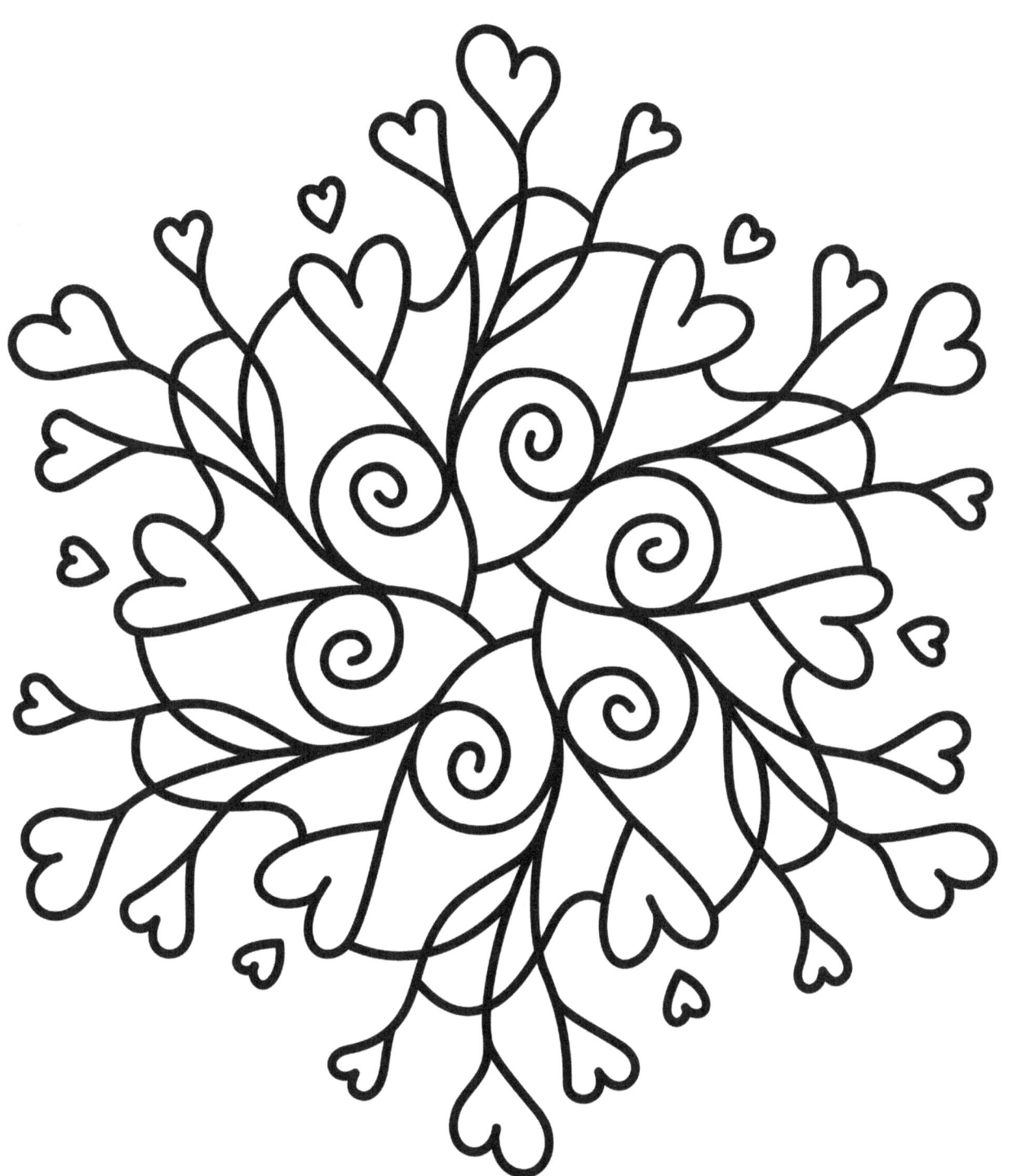

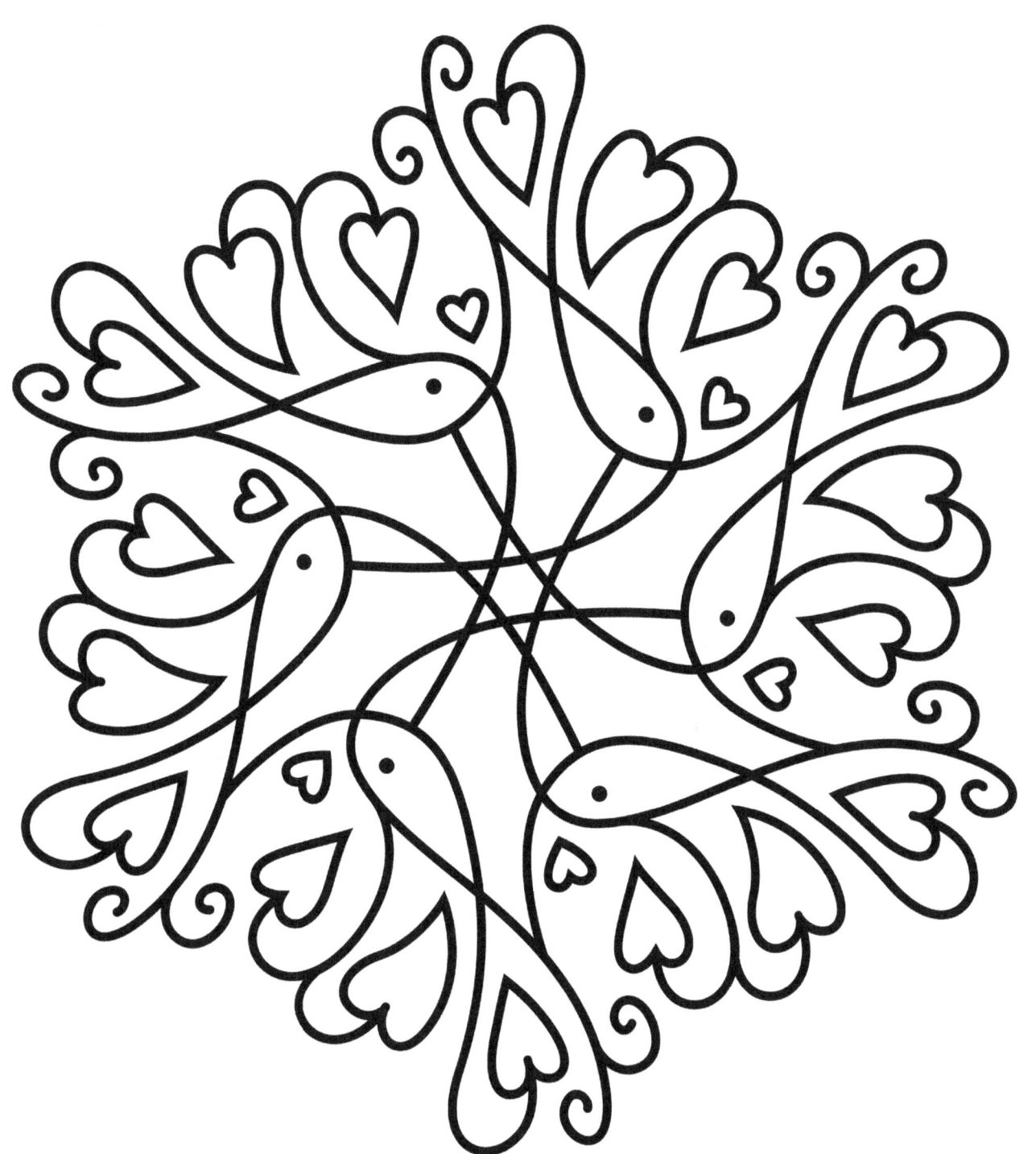

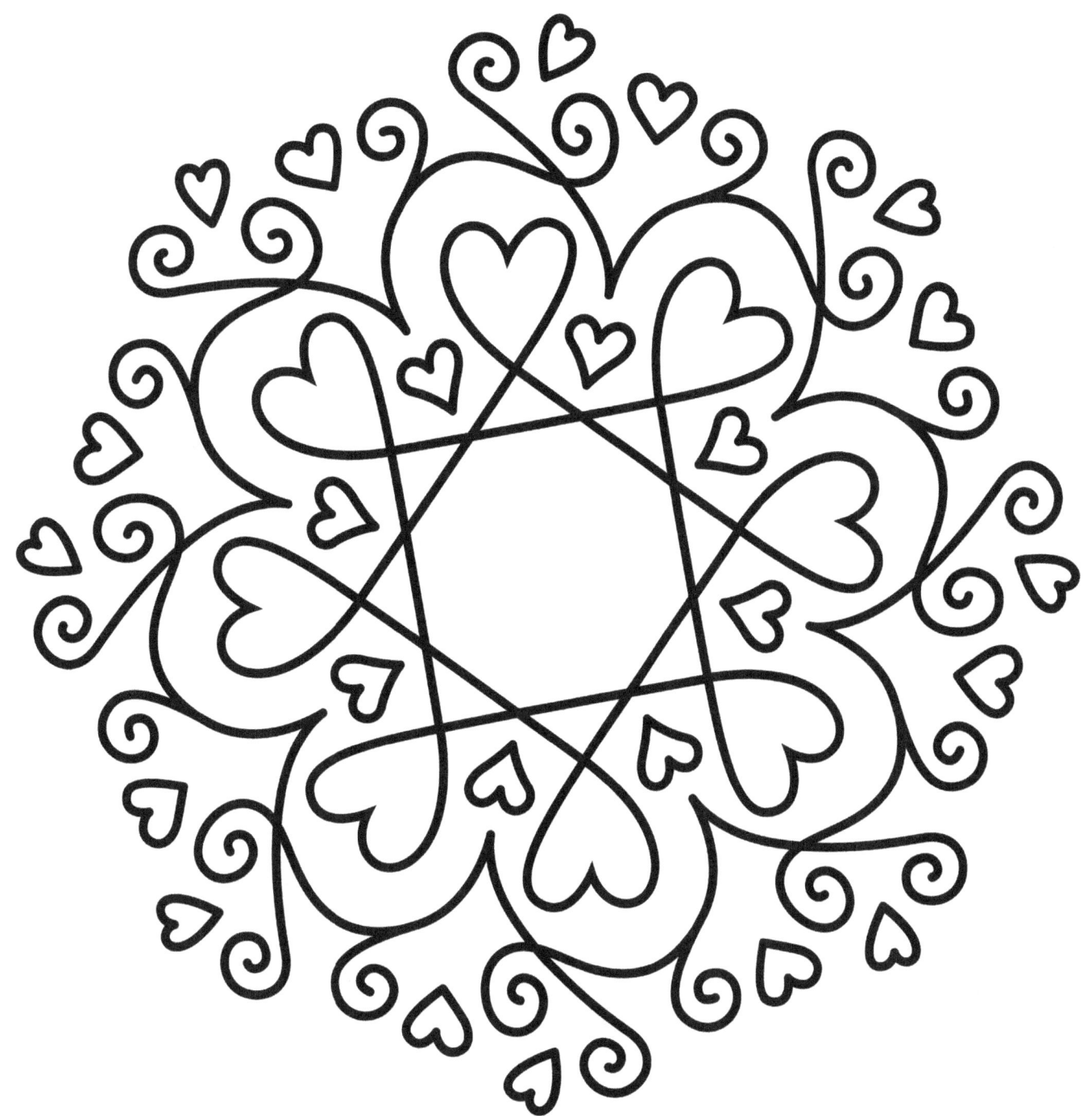

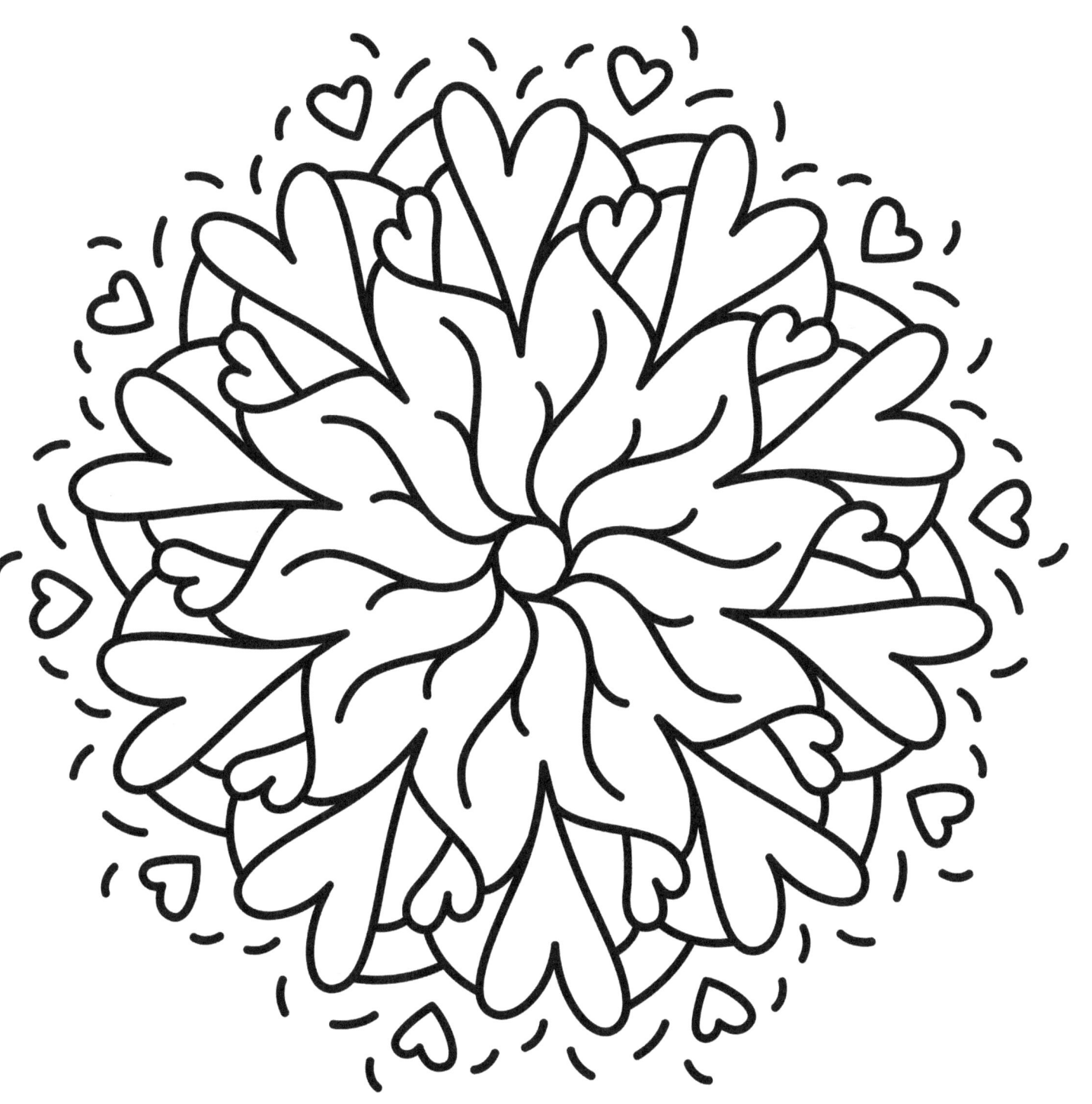

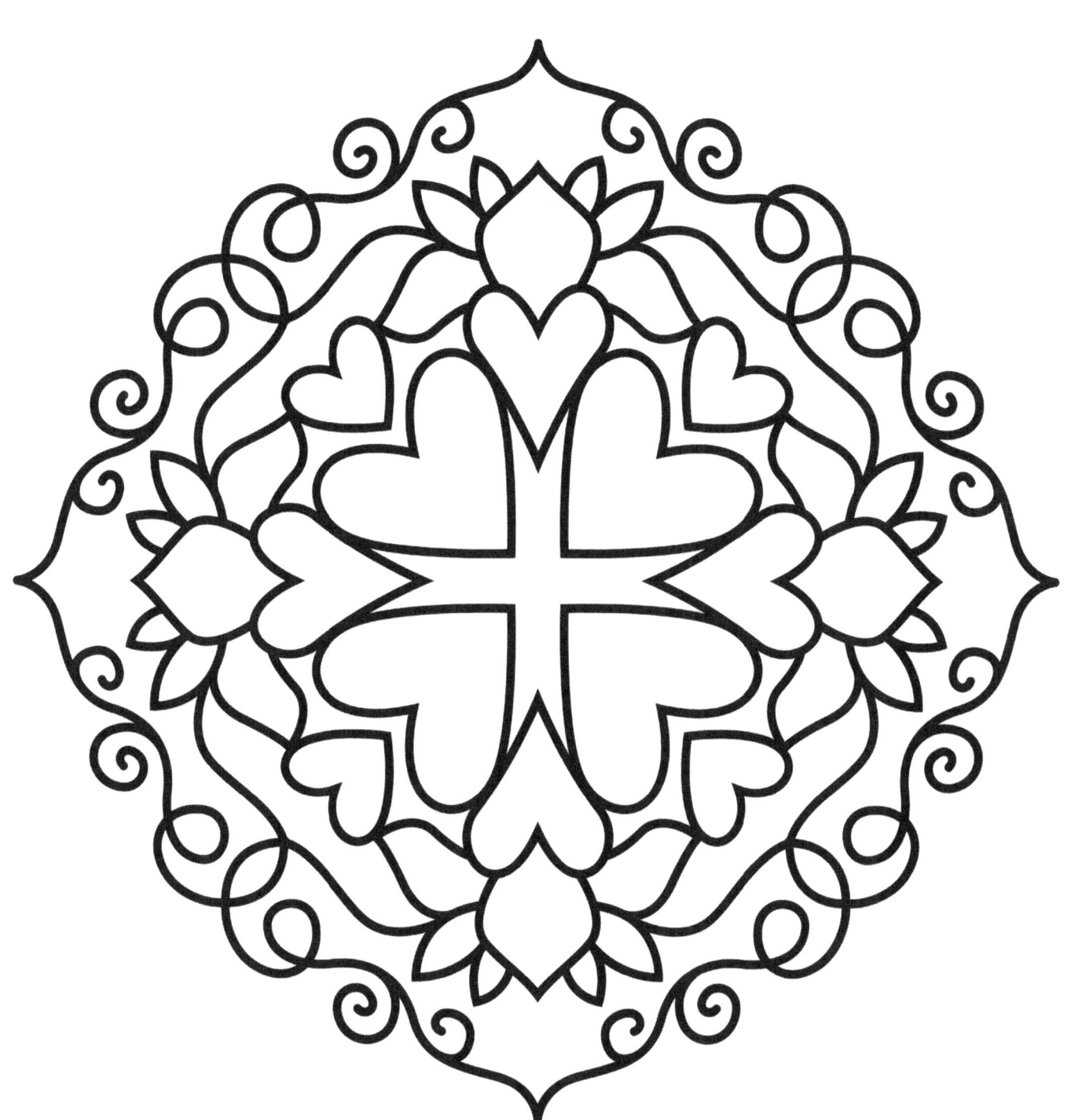

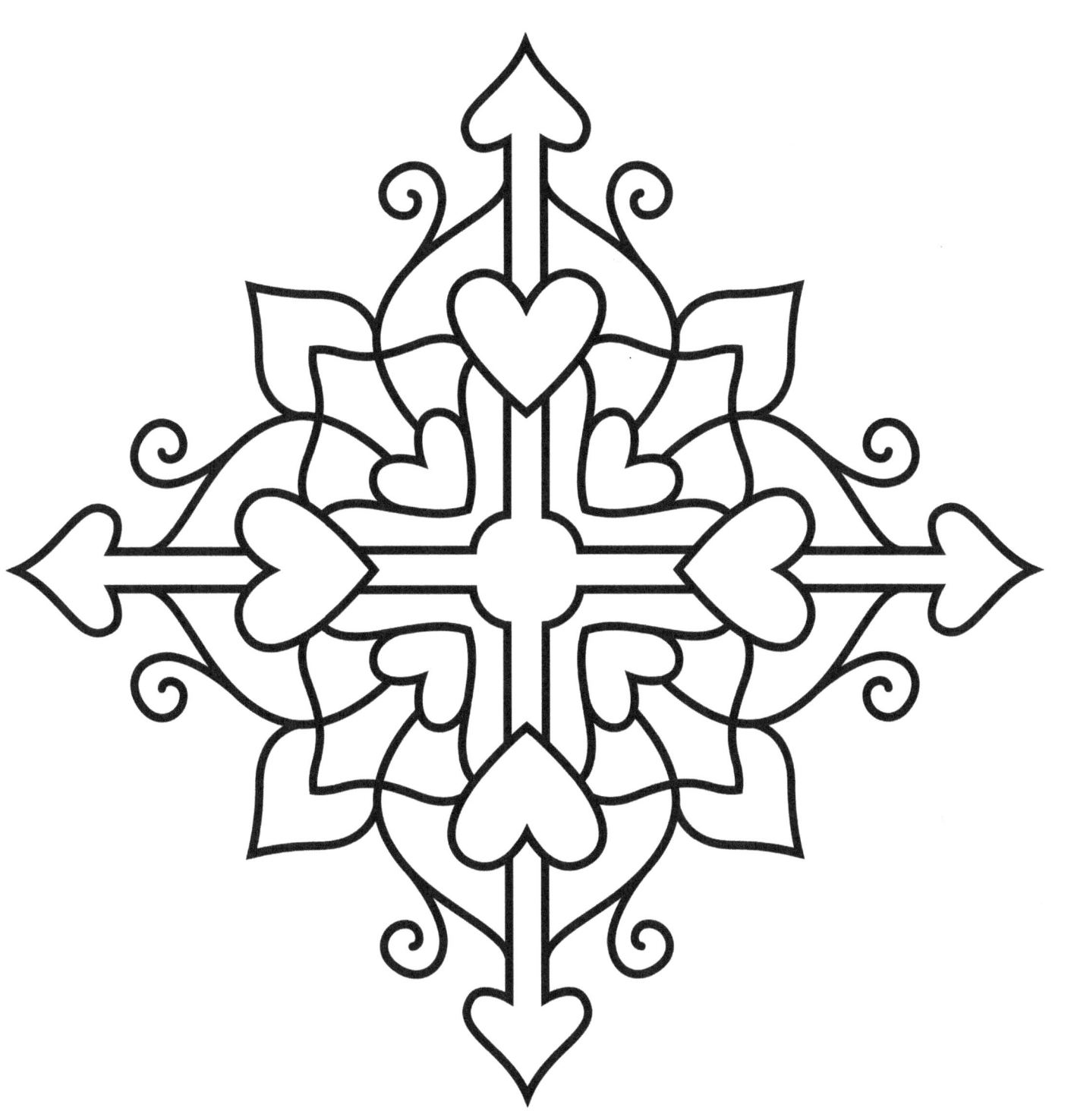

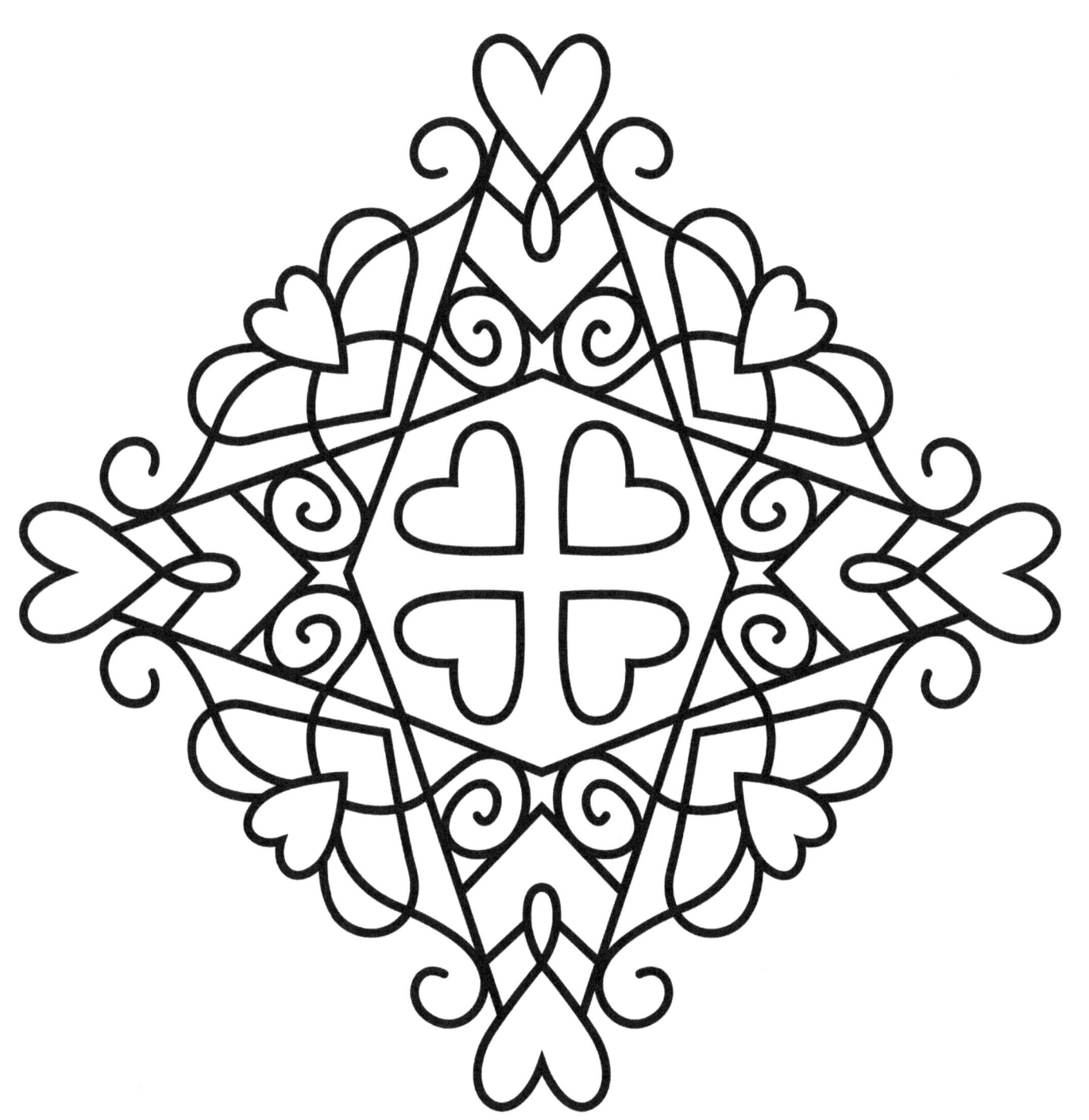

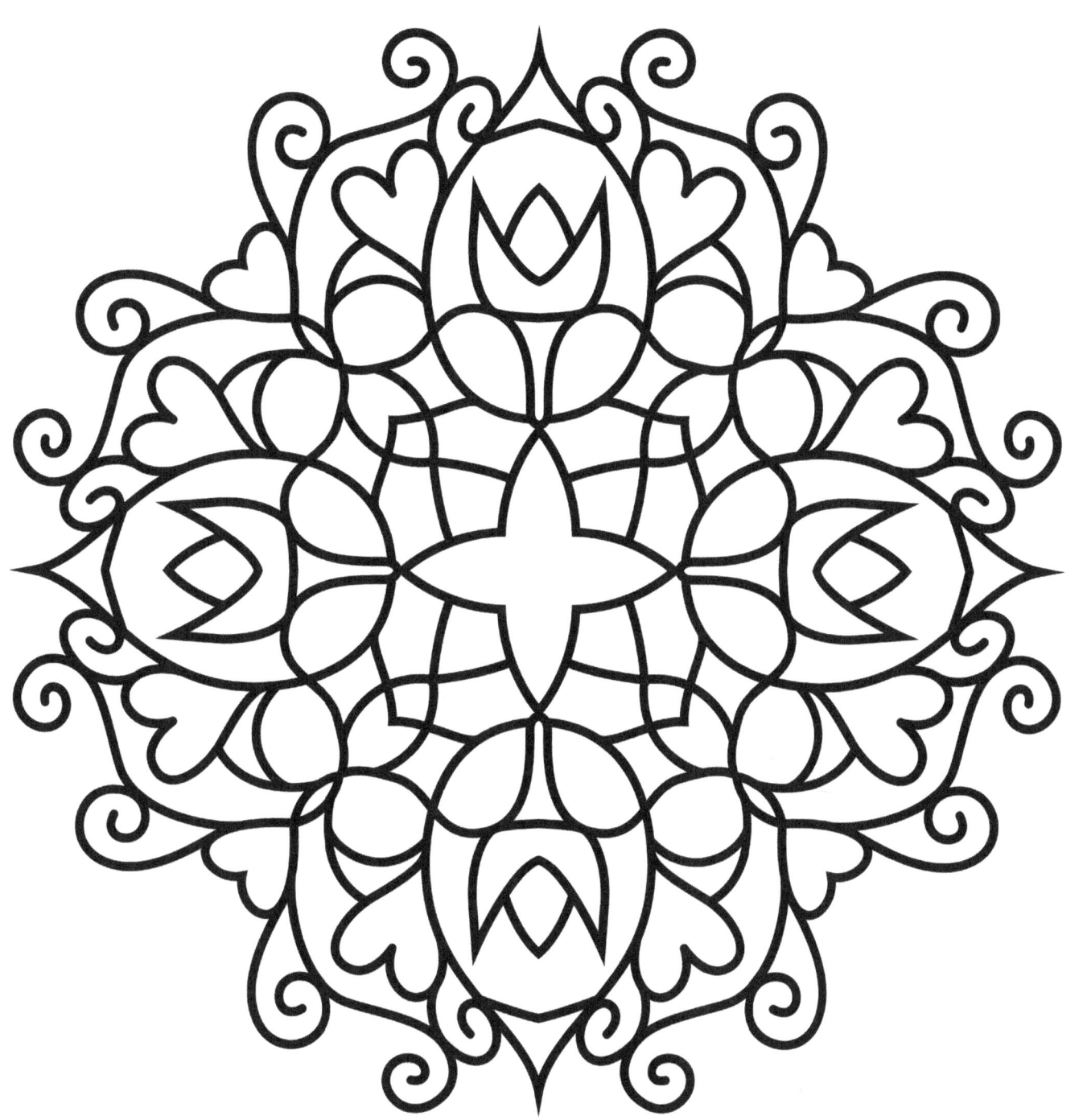

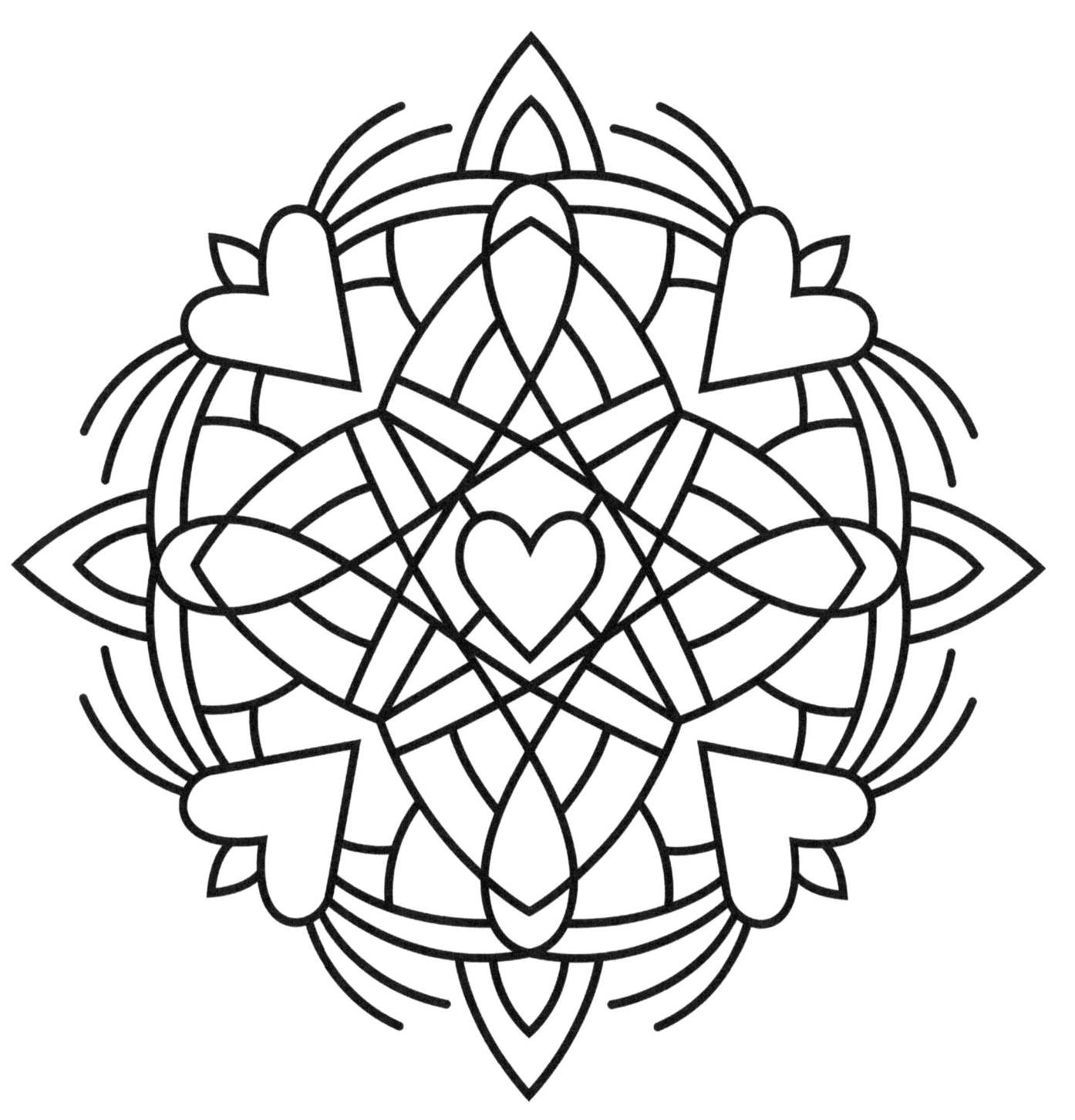

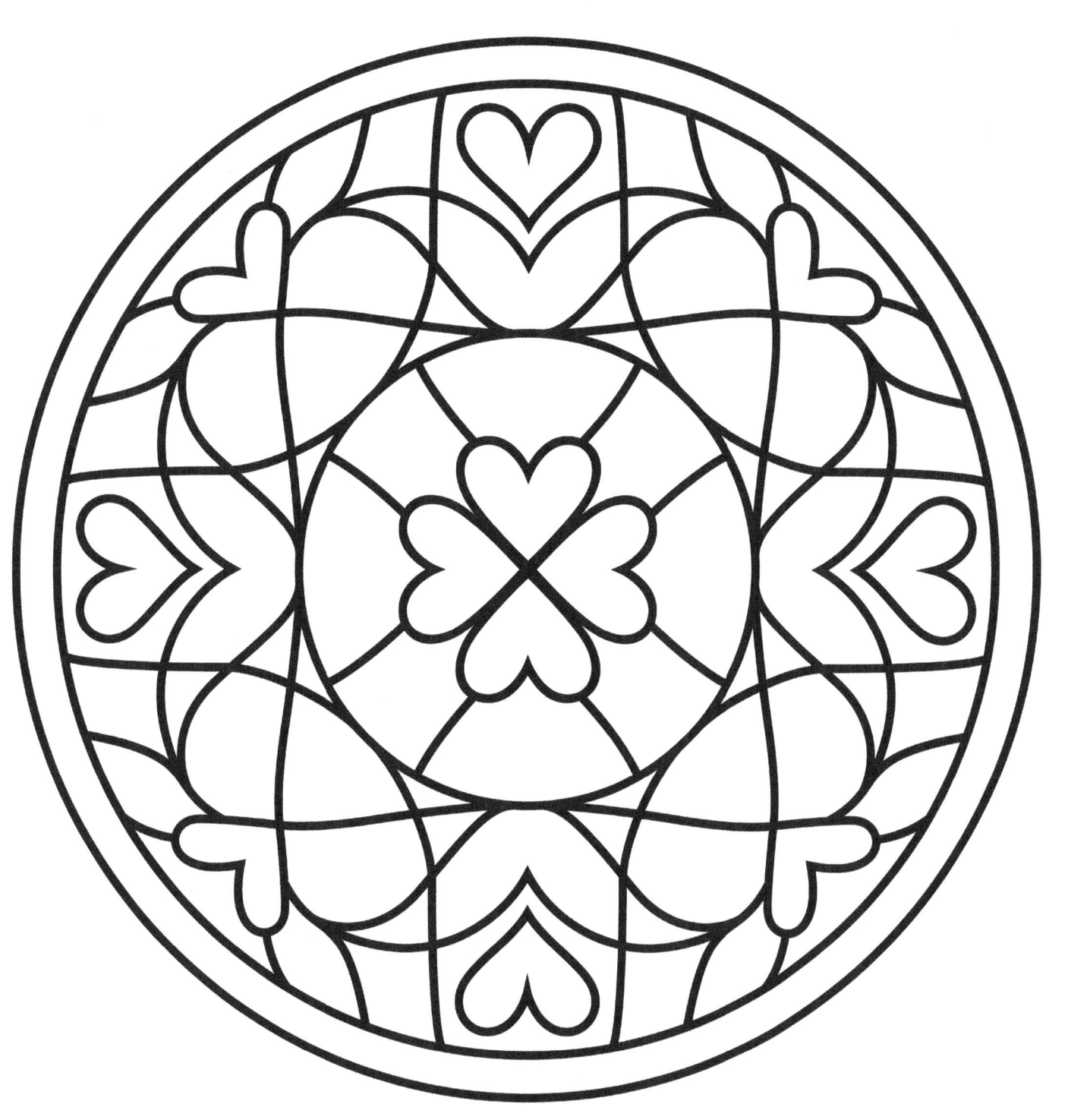

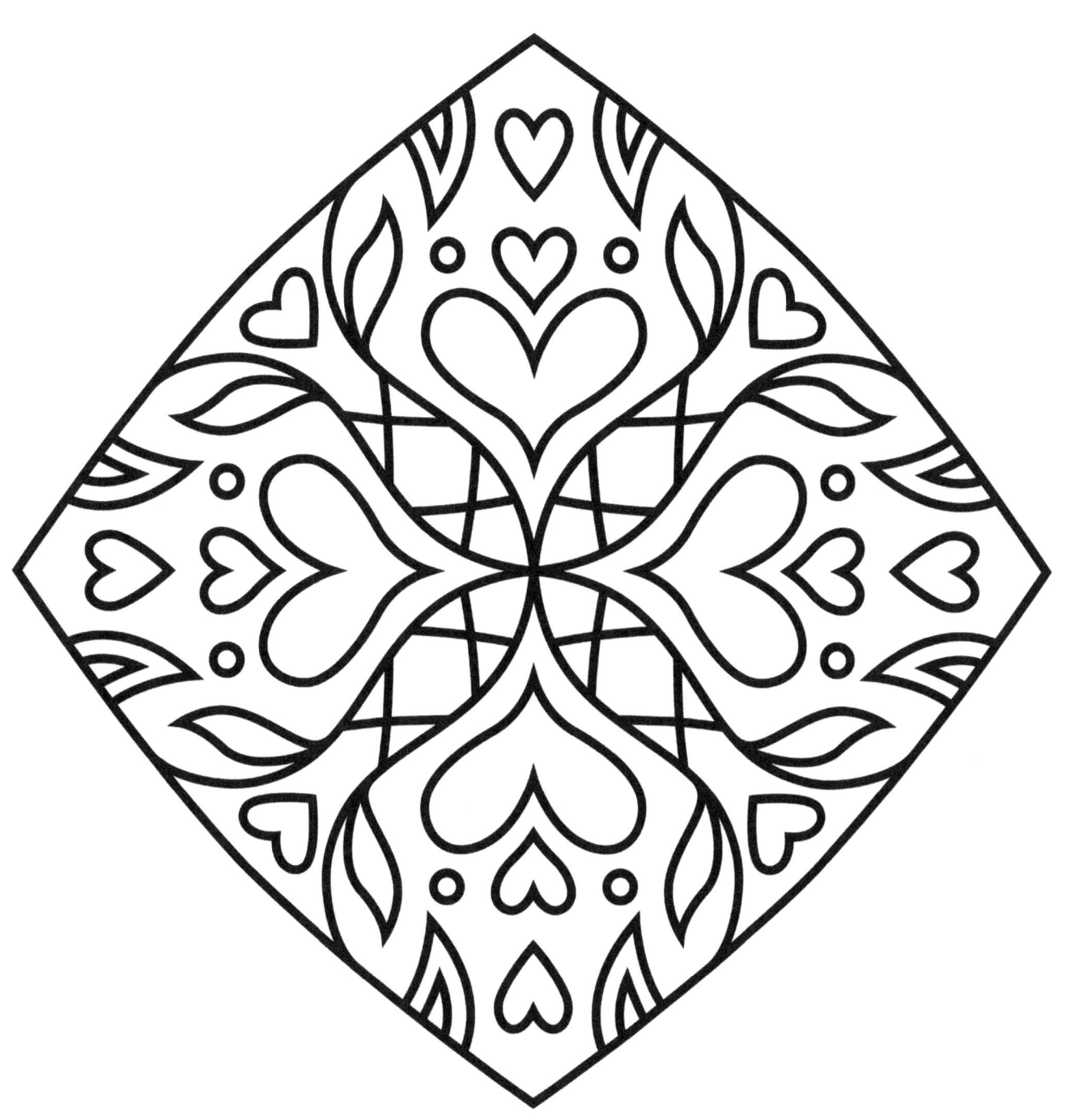

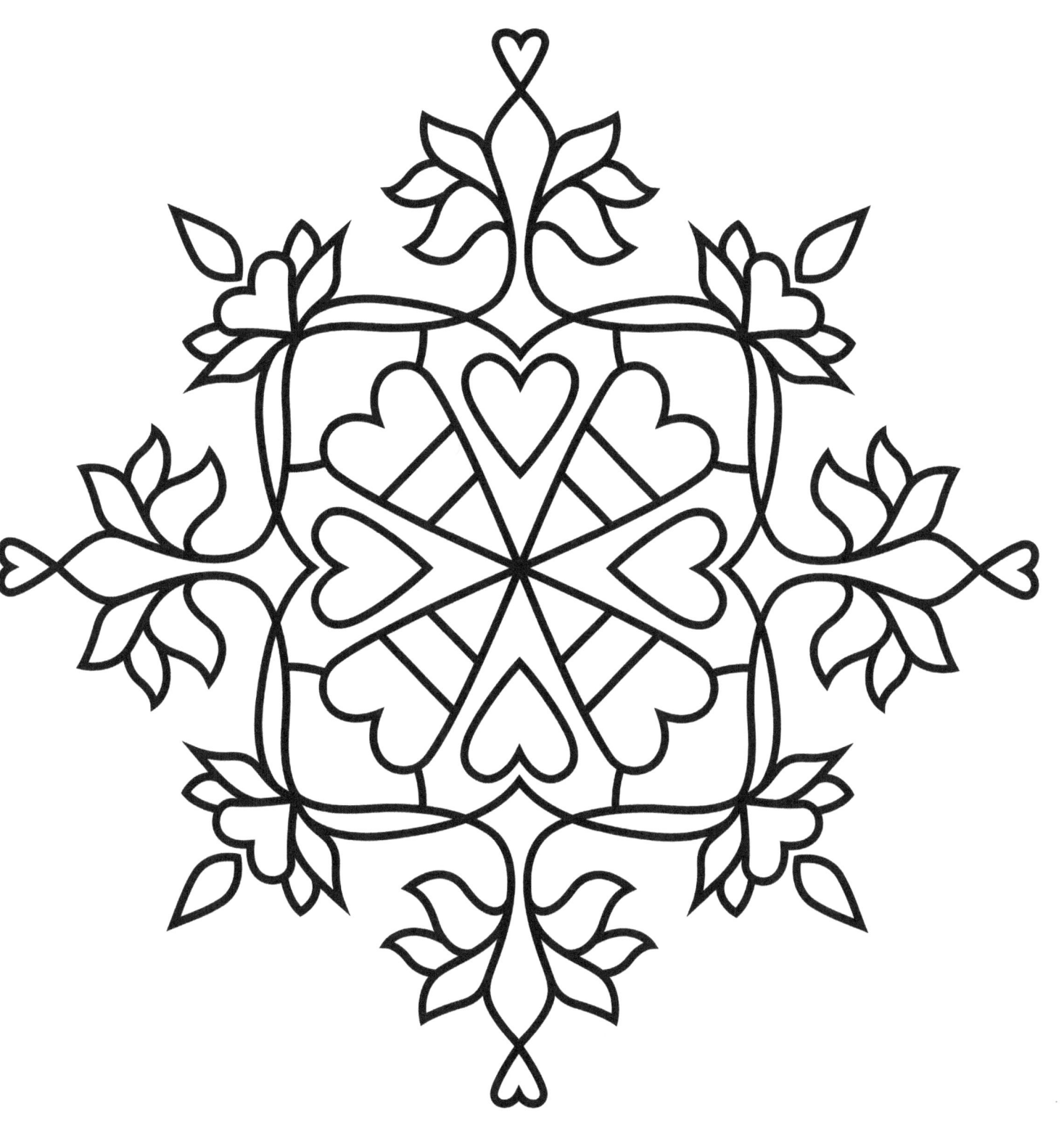

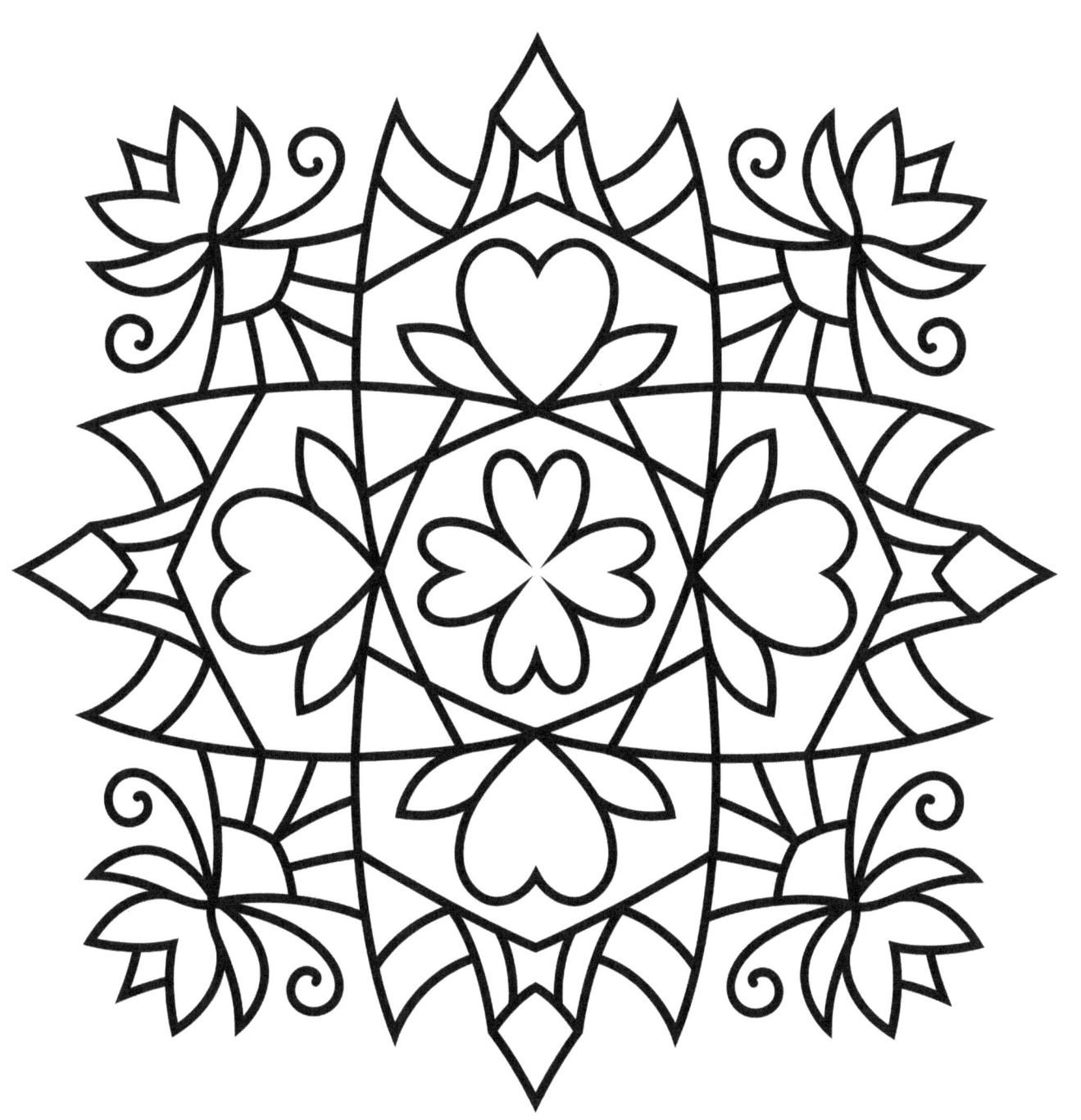

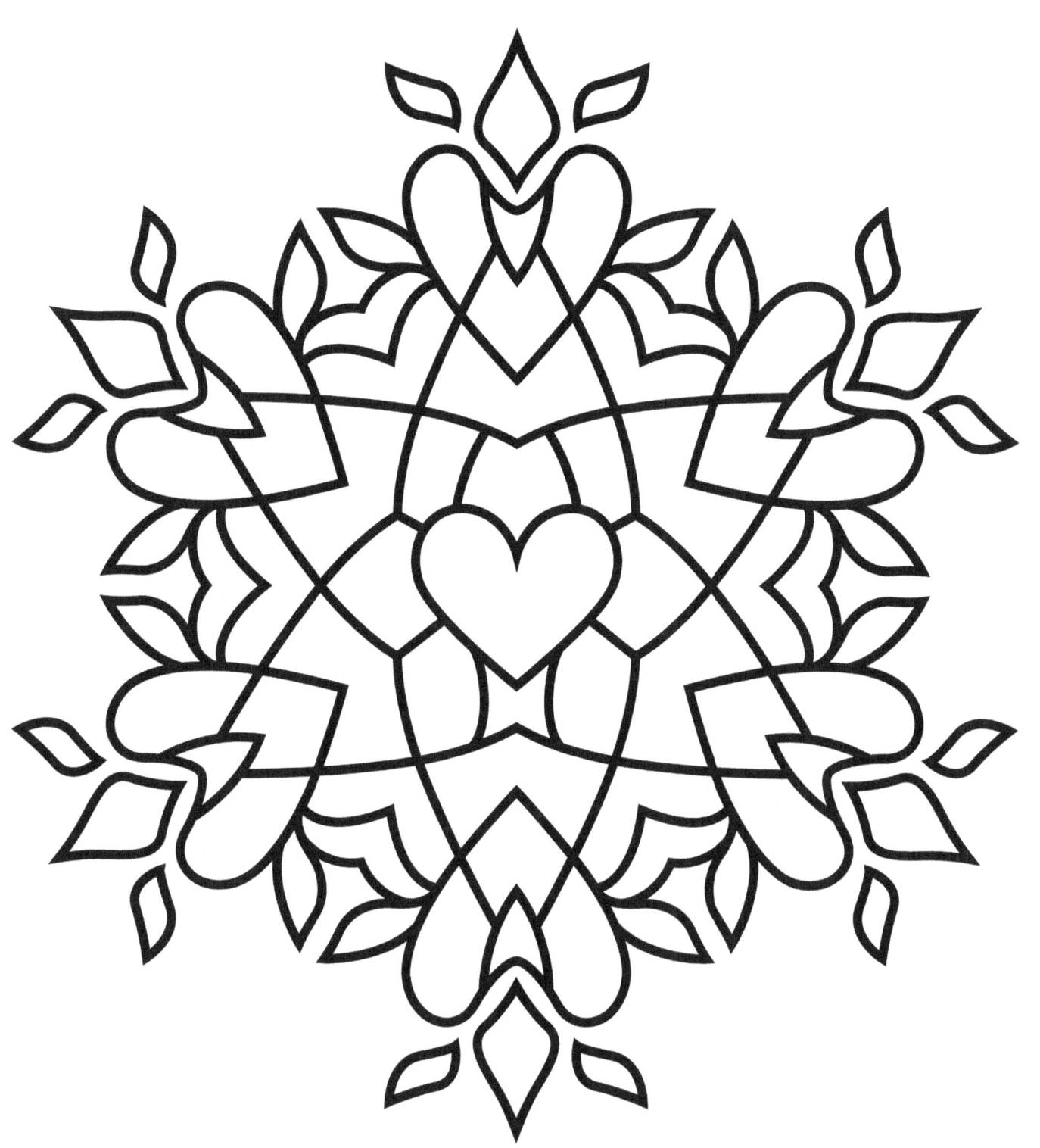

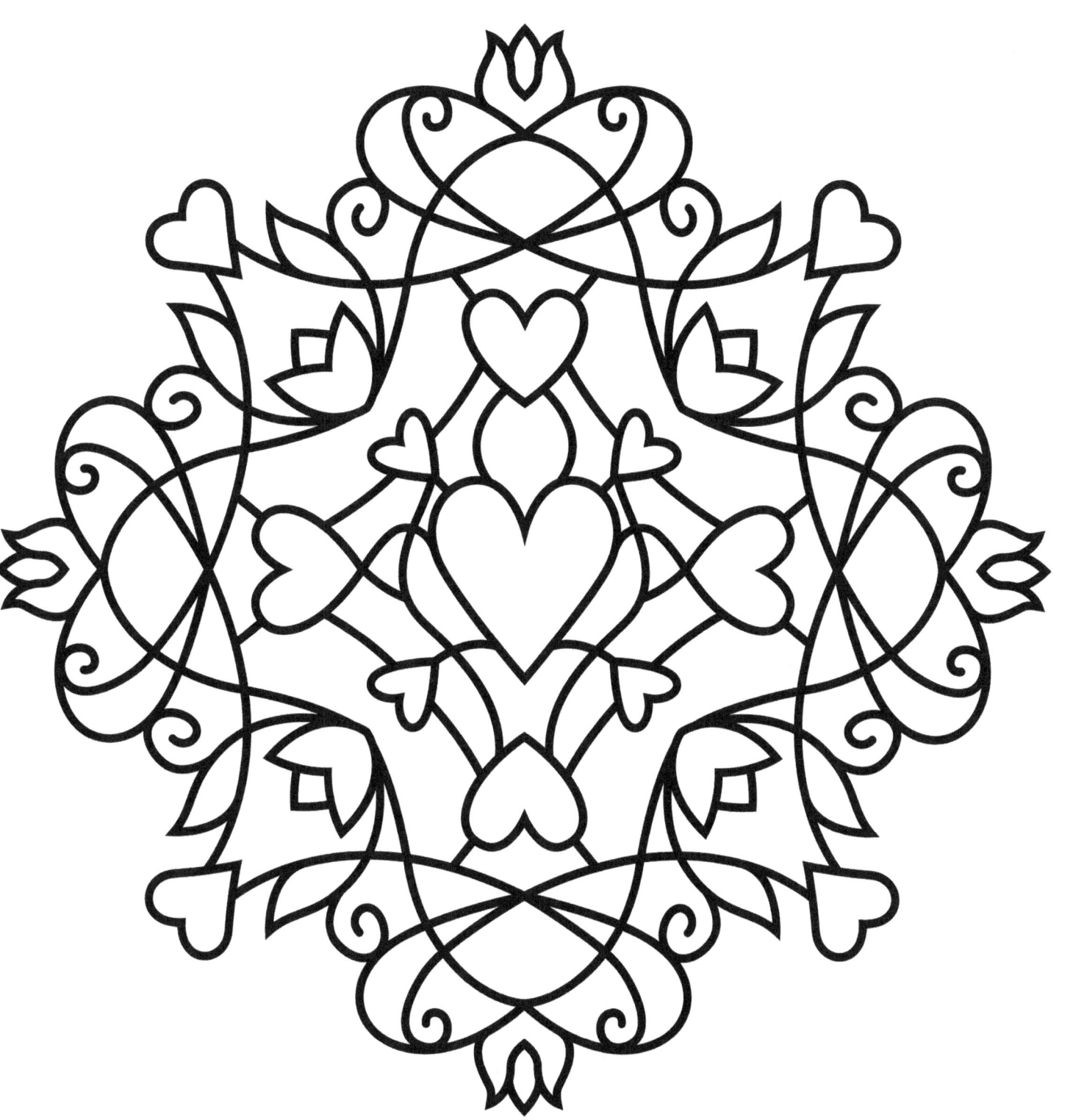

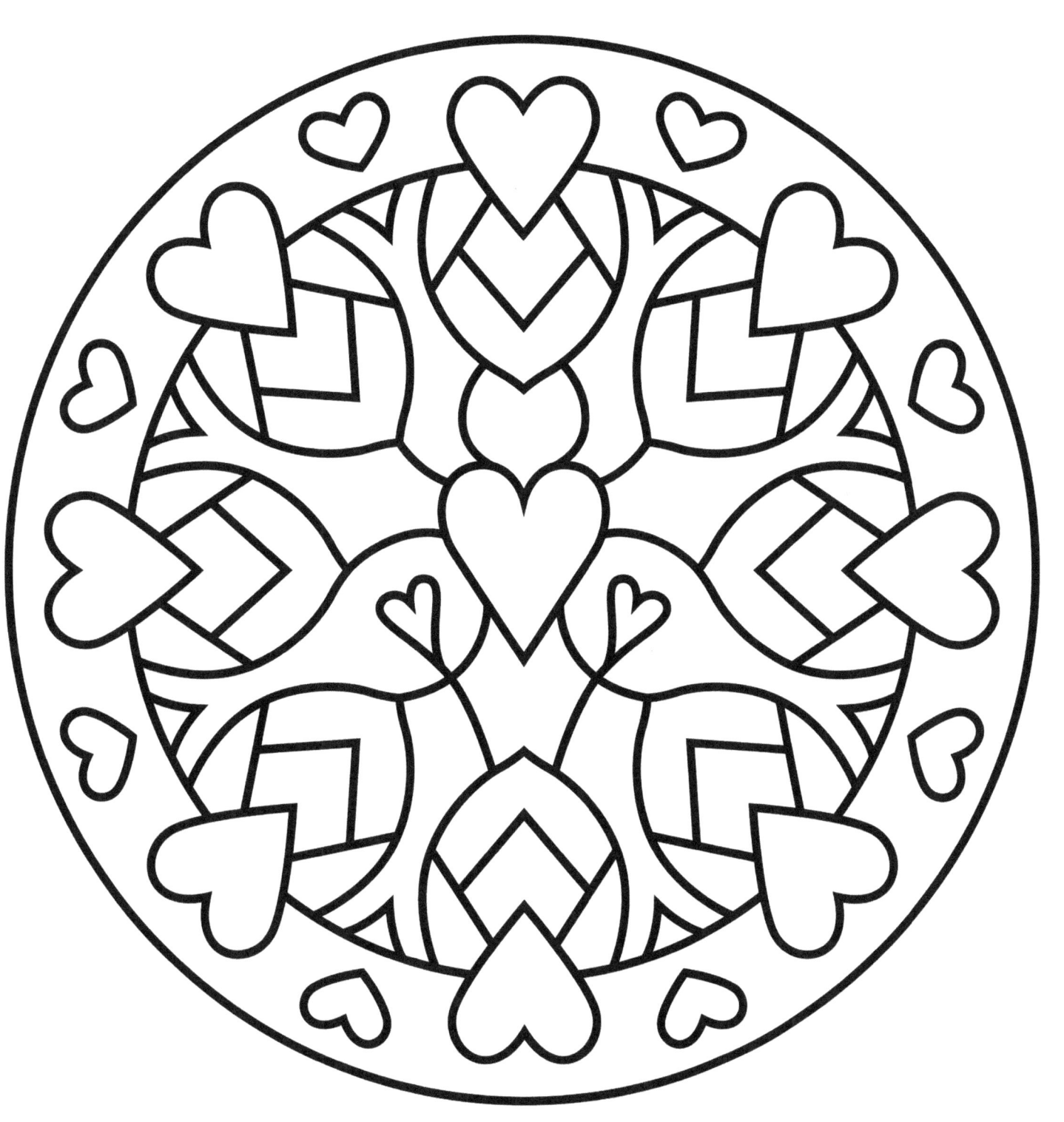

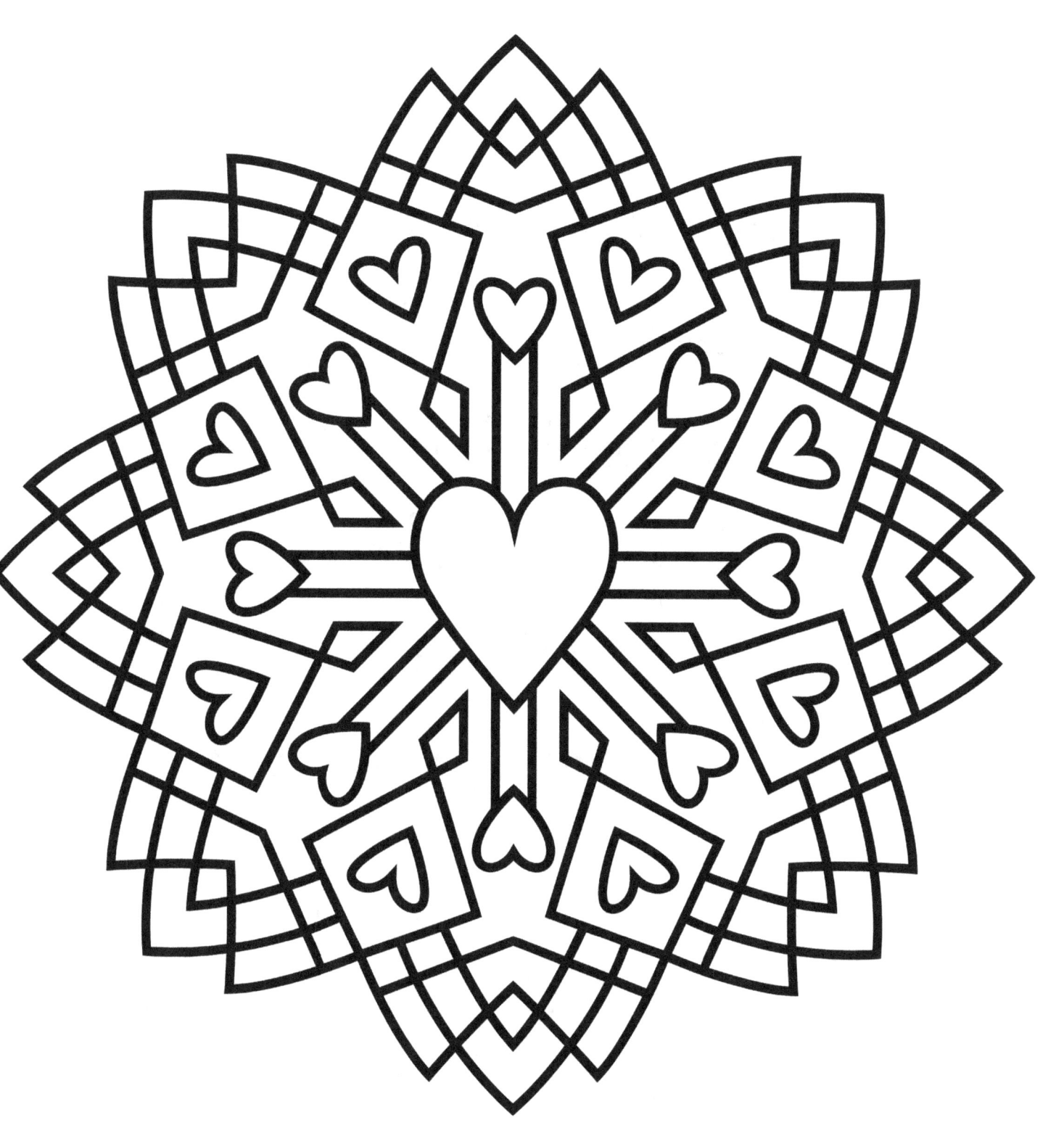

We hope you enjoyed our book

As a small family company, your feedback is very important to us. Please let us know how you like our book at:
drcipcom@gmail.com

Skypi